TWENTY-EIGHT
BOTTLES
AROUND THE BAY

TWENTY-EIGHT
BOTTLES
AROUND THE BAY

TEN GOURMET DINNERS FOR PEOPLE
WITH NO TIME AND NO SPACE

MARGARET SHARPE

ILLUSTRATIONS BY PIM

The BOSTON
MILLS PRESS

© Copyright Margaret Sharpe, 1998

All rights reserved. No part of this publication may be reproduced or transmitted in any form or by any means, electronic or mechanical, including photocopying, recording, or any information storage and retrieval system, without permission in writing from the publisher.

Published in 1998 by
Boston Mills Press
132 Main Street
Erin, Ontario
N0B 1T0
www.boston-mills.on.ca

An affiliate of Stoddart Publishing Co. Limited
34 Lesmill Road
Toronto, Ontario, Canada
M3B 2T6

Distributed in Canada by
General Distribution Services Limited
30 Lesmill Road
Toronto, Canada M3B 2T6
Tel 416-445-3333
Fax 416-445-5967
Canadian Telebook S1150391
e-mail gdsinc@genpub.com

Distributed in the United States by
General Distribution Services Inc.
85 River Rock Drive, Suite 202
Buffalo, New York 14207-2170
Toll-free 1-800-805-1083
Toll-free fax 1-800-481-6207
PUBNET 6307949
e-mail gdsinc.genpub.com

02 01 00 99 98   1 2 3 4 5

Cataloging in Publication Data
Sharpe, Margaret, 1959-
    Twenty-eight bottles around the Bay

ISBN 1-55046-239-3

1. Cookery, Marine. 2. Dinners and dining. 3. Menus.
I. Title.

TX840.M7S52 1998   641.5'753   98-930337-3

Illustrations by PIM
Design by Mary Firth

Printed in Canada

CONTENTS

Acknowledgments 6

Introduction 7

The Essential Galley 8

The Menus 10

Cooking Tips 61

Wine Wisdom 67

Shopping List 73

Recipe Index 76

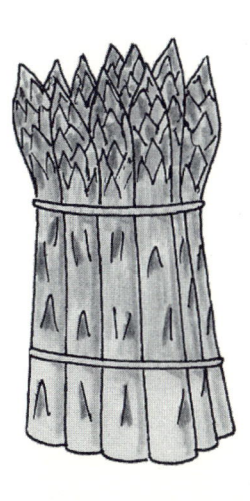

The strength that lies in the hull of a ship, the beauty of sails, the surge of water, the taste of the sea, the touch of the wind on our faces, and even the little simple pleasures of eating, and drinking, and sleeping, all these we share with delight and understanding, because of the happiness we have in one another.

— Daphne du Maurier
Frenchman's Creek

ACKNOWLEDGMENTS

This cookbook is dedicated with fond memories to James Greenshields, our sommelier at sea, and his wife Elizabeth, cruise director and chief dishwasher, who were our intrepid sailing companions aboard *King James Version* when the idea was germinated. James is a gourmet cook, and we had a good time bouncing ideas and menus off each other, even though the weather stank most of the time.

And with grateful thanks to my husband, David, who skippered us safely through some of the worst weather Georgian Bay has to offer, thus making the whole thing possible.

The original version of *Twenty-Eight Bottles Around the Bay* was sold at a gala charity auction to raise funds for the Canadian Progress Club. It would never have come into being without the unfailing patience and professionalism of two people — Inge Tysoe, my computer consultant, and Pim, the artist — who also happen to be my parents. Thanks, Mum and Dad, for everything, from my first introduction to sailing until now.

Here's to the wind that blows, a ship that goes, and the lass that loved a sailor!

— *Traditional Royal Navy toast*

INTRODUCTION

A few summers ago, my husband, David, and I sailed around Georgian Bay in our yawl, the *King James Version*, with a couple of newlywed friends, James and Elizabeth, and some of the worst midsummer weather we had ever seen, even in Canada.

Planning for the trip, in the spacious comfort of our own kitchens, was an exhilarating task. As we would be sailing in a watery wilderness, anchoring out at night, we would have to take along food and drink sufficient for ten days. But what we were preparing was no store of hardtack and water. We spent weeks planning the menus down to the last detail, including wine and aperitifs, all the while taking into account our limited facilities — a galley smaller than Mrs. Beeton's backside, a cantankerous kerosene stove, and two square feet of stainless steel counter. Electricity would be a distantly remembered luxury; the only refrigeration we would have would consist of an icebox that seemed to swallow whatever went into it like a black hole.

We sailed from five every morning until dusk, the men being adamant that we complete our circumnavigation come high water, groundings, storms, or any of the ills that beset even the most carefully planned sails. That left us, after each day's battle against bruising winds, glaring sun, or, more often, pelting rain, with monstrous appetites but little energy left for cooking.

One disastrous evening, a fine Chardonnay was ruined by soapsuds in the glasses and our carefully prepared grain-fed chicken breasts were reduced to compressed sawdust in between my pulling down the sails and dropping the anchor. James and I had a good many words, and I began to make serious notes about how to cook with no space and no time.

All of the recipes here were developed and tested in the confines of the *King James Version* galley or in the equally Lilliputian kitchen of the mobile home in which I lived and worked for seven years. Shortcuts are used whever possible, with suggestions for alternative ingredients, taking into account factors such as seasonal availability, personal taste, and food allergies. You will find explanations about less familiar ingredients and methods in the "Cooking Tips" section. Each menu serves four; the recipes can be adjusted for any number of people. Many of the appetizers, soups and salads can also stand alone as simple meals.

The title of this book is inspired by the fine vintage wines that cheered many a companionable evening in the cabin of the *King James Version*, as we lingered over dinner in the glow of the gently swaying oil lamp, with the strains of Mozart or Pachelbel rising softly above the slapping of waves against the hull. I have included a section on "Wine Wisdom" at the end of the book because, as the great gastronome, Anthelme Brillat-Savarin, said, "A meal without wine is like a day without sunshine."

A place for everything and everything in its place.

— Isabella Mary Beeton
The Book of Household Management

THE ESSENTIAL GALLEY

Space is at a premium on any sailboat, particularly in the galley. Every square inch is given up grudgingly, only to items of essential importance. Needless to say, organization is vital, not only because of space restrictions, but also because there is no room for waste and no way to get hold of anything you forgot to put on your shopping list the day before. When you're out at anchor, you can't just pop down to the local convenience store for butter or cream.

For all these reasons, cooking on board ship is great training for working efficiently in any kitchen. The following are a few suggestions for the utensils and gadgets that I find essential to the efficient preparation of meals. All are readily available, extremely durable, and will enhance not only your enjoyment in cooking but also the results of your labors.

CHOPPING BOARDS: Wooden chopping boards have been unfairly maligned of late. There remains no more useful, practical or, indeed, sanitary material for the preparation of food than the humble old chopping block — unbreakable, forgiving, and cleaner than plastic. Wooden boards need no more care than to be wiped clean and allowed to dry thoroughly after each use. I keep one board, appropriately pig-shaped, exclusively for cutting raw meat. Occasionally, I scrub it down with a little bleach.

GARLIC PRESS: The garlic press is one of the most essential kitchen utensils. The Susi, made by Zyliss and available from any kitchen shop, will last you a lifetime. Just pop in a garlic clove (no need to peel it) and press. It takes all the horror out of using fresh garlic. I also use mine for mincing shallots, which is so tedious with a knife, and for producing small amounts of onion juice to flavor dips and sauces.

GRATERS: Heavy steel graters, ranging from medium to very coarse, are invaluable for grating potatoes, root vegetables, and hard cheeses, especially Parmesan. All my graters have come from antique or junk shops, but good modern steel graters are available from a few speciality kitchen shops and restaurant equipment suppliers. A Parmesan grater is handy for the table; Zyliss makes a good one.

By far the most useful fine grater I have is from Lee Valley Tools. The Micro-Plane Rigid Flat Rasp Blade, made of high quality stainless steel, is actually a woodworking tool, but there is nothing better for grating zest, whole nutmeg and fresh ginger, or for reducing garlic cloves to a paste.

KITCHEN SCALE: A scale is the most accurate and least messy way to measure bulk ingredients. Mine is by Farberware; it is lightweight and has a deep plastic weighing pan, which, turned over, becomes a lid, allowing for compact storage.

KNIVES: Sabatier makes the best, but Henkel's are also good. The important thing is to keep your knives sharp, which means touching them up with a hand-held grinding stone, a sharpening steel, or on the unglazed bottom of a ceramic mug (really, it works wonders) every time you use them. Dull knives force you to use too much pressure when cutting and chopping, which is dangerous and will spoil the appearance of fragile foods. Wipe your knives dry immediately after every use; never put them in the dishwasher.

POTS AND PANS: My favorite material is cast iron. It is cheap, durable, and practical, and is simple to clean and maintain. It heats evenly and is excellent for rapid searing, simmering, broiling, and long, slow cooking. Properly seasoned cast iron also provides the best non-wearing non-stick surface of all cookware, allowing you to reduce the use of fats in your cooking. It is practically indispensable in searing meat properly, as it is the only cookware you can allow to get hot enough to carbonise the surface of the meat, a process which produces dark, rich, flavorful gravy. The only disadvantage to cast iron is the weight. On the other hand, if you spend your evenings hefting these pots and pans around the kitchen, you will no longer need to cart about wrist weights on your morning power walks.

My essential galley has four eight-inch skillets, one ten-inch and one twelve-inch, all with oven-proof handles. The small ones are ideal for quick toasting of nuts, pan-frying for one to four people, and making individual omelettes. All of these skillets make excellent roasting and broiling pans for meats, vegetables, and fish, and are much easier to clean and store than the roasting pans provided with most ovens. In addition to the skillets, I also have a large Dutch oven for long, slow roasting.

Seasoning cast iron is simple. Wipe it well with cooking oil and then leave it in a moderate oven for an hour or two. Your pans will improve with use. Never scrub with detergent or abrasive cleaners; instead, soak, if necessary, then wipe clean with a dishcloth. Give them an occasional wipe with oil after they are dry.

Enamel-coated iron can also be useful, especially for acidic dishes containing tomatoes. Always try to buy cookware with oven-proof handles. Although it means you will have to use potholders, it is an immense convenience for last-minute broiling or for keeping foods warm in the oven.

STAINLESS STEEL STRAINER: Useful, of course, for draining vegetables and canned fruits, but also in place of a blender in the production of purées. Push the soup or fruit mixture through with a wooden spoon. Invaluable aboard a boat with no electricity.

WOODEN SPOONS: Vital for stirring and tasting, they will not scratch your cookware or burn your tongue. For care, see **Chopping Boards**.

TWENTY-EIGHT BOTTLES AROUND THE BAY ⚓ 9

THE MENUS

MENU ONE 12
Wild Mushroom Soup
Endive and Radish Salad with Rose Petals and Dill Cream
Fillet of Sole with Pink Peppercorn and Tarragon Butter
Peppered Strawberries and Crème Fraîche

MENU TWO 17
Cardamom-Scented Apple Soup
Asparagus Spears with Egg Mousse and Caviar
Grilled Salmon with Fresh Herb Salsa
Spiced Banana and Rum Crêpes

MENU THREE 22
Seafood Coquilles
Chilled Avocado Soup
Medallions of Pork Tenderloin with Calvados
Grapes Gervaise

MENU FOUR 27
Spring Green Soup
Tomato Flowers with Stilton
Veal in Mushroom and Shallot Cream
Pots-de-Crème with Cointreau

MENU FIVE 32
Clear Leek Soup
Smoked Salmon with Black Pepper Crème Fraîche
Rack of Lamb with Mustard and Rosemary Pesto
Syllabub

MENU SIX 37
Garlic Soup

Chèvre-Stuffed Pears with Cumin Sauce

Savory Crêpes with Herb-Seasoned Filling

Raspberry Fool

MENU SEVEN 42
Broiled Roquefort

Chilled Herb and Parsley Soup

Champagne Chicken

Pound Cake Croustades with Brandied Fruit

MENU EIGHT 47
Sea Scallop Soup

Zucchini in Olive Oil with Toasted Pine Nuts and Golden Raisins

Pepper-Crusted Beef Tenderloin in Black Olive Butter

Peach Chiffon

MENU NINE 52
Crudités with Herbed Dijon Vinaigrette

Braised Beef in Red Wine

Roasted Camembert with Raspberry Coulis and Walnuts

MENU TEN 56
Chick-Pea Soup with Aïoli

Fennel and Orange Salad

Agnolotti in Roasted Red Pepper Sauce

Hot Glazed Fruit

MENU ONE

Wild Mushroom Soup

❧

Endive and Radish Salad with Rose Petals
and Dill Cream

❧

Filet of Sole with Pink Peppercorn
and Tarragon Butter

❧

Peppered Strawberries and Crème Fraîche

The ideal base for this soup is a game bird stock such as pheasant, goose or duck, which, unless you make it yourself, can be difficult to find. Otherwise, the blend of chicken broth, beef consommé and port or Madeira wine is a reasonable substitute.

WILD MUSHROOM SOUP

- 1/4 pound mixed variety of mushrooms (such as crimini, shiitake, and oyster), finely chopped
- 2–3 tablespoons butter (optional)
- 1/4 cup port or Madeira wine
- 1 10-ounce can condensed chicken broth
- 1 10-ounce can condensed beef consommé
- 1/2 cup port or Madeira wine

1 In a small heavy skillet over medium heat, melt the butter. Add the mushrooms and cook gently until softened, about five minutes. Increase heat to high, add the wine and reduce to a glaze, about one minute. If you don't wish to use butter, cook the mushrooms directly in the wine over medium-high heat.

2 Meanwhile, in a medium heavy saucepan over moderate heat, bring the chicken broth, consommé, and half cup of wine to a boil. Simmer until the mushrooms are ready. Season to taste with salt and freshly ground black pepper.

3 Divide the mushrooms between four warmed soup bowls. Ladle the simmering broth over them. Garnish with chopped chives or green onions.

TIPS:
For a rich touch, top each bowl with a spoonful of crème fraîche.

Soup is to a dinner what a portico or a peristyle is to a building…it must be made in such a manner as to set the tone of the whole banquet, in the same way as the overture of an opera makes known the subject of the work.

— Grimod de la Reynière

TWENTY-EIGHT BOTTLES AROUND THE BAY   13

Rose petals add a fragrant, festive touch to this salad; don't be tempted to leave them out. If you have none in your garden, bunches of four or five buds are available at most supermarkets for a reasonable price (make sure they are pesticide free). Use the extras to decorate the table.

If you are allergic to dairy products, substitute 1/4 cup olive oil for the yogurt and mayonnaise.

ENDIVE AND RADISH SALAD WITH ROSE PETALS AND DILL CREAM

1/4 cup sour cream or plain yogurt

1/4 cup mayonnaise

1/4 cup chopped fresh dill

Juice of half a lemon

2 heads Belgian endive

4 radishes, thinly sliced or grated

Petals from a red rosebud

1. In a small bowl, blend the sour cream, mayonnaise, dill and lemon juice. Season to taste with salt and freshly ground black pepper. The dressing may be prepared a day ahead.

2. Rinse the rose petals gently. Allow them to dry on a paper towel.

3. Cut the bottom off each of the lettuce heads. Slice the heads crosswise into thirds. Separate the leaves and divide them among four salad plates. Drizzle with the dill cream. Sprinkle the radishes and rose petals over the lettuce. Garnish with more chopped fresh dill or with a sprig of dill on the side.

TIPS:
Crumbled feta or chèvre is a nice addition to the salad.

For a main luncheon or light supper dish, add cooked baby shrimp, shredded crab meat, chunks of cooked lobster meat, white tuna, cooked sliced sea scallops or whole bay scallops.

A rose is sweeter in the bud than full-blown.

— John Lyly
Euphues and His England

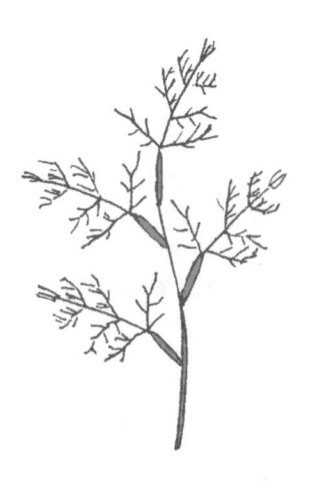

The butter sauce is good with any delicately flavored fish, but you can also try it with boneless, skinless chicken breasts, pan-fried white veal, or boneless pork loin chops. If you prefer, the fish can be pan fried instead of poached. For a low-fat meal, substitute the poaching liquid for the butter in the sauce.

FILLET OF SOLE WITH PINK PEPPERCORN AND TARRAGON BUTTER

About 8 large fresh spinach leaves or any dark green salad leaves

Butter (optional)

1/2 cup dry white vermouth

1 10-ounce can condensed chicken broth

4 sole fillets (about 6 ounces per person)

1/2 cup butter

1 tablespoon crushed pink peppercorns

1/4 cup chopped fresh tarragon, or 2 tablespoons dried

Juice of 1 lemon

1 Wash the salad greens, but do not dry them. In a large heavy skillet over medium heat, in a little melted butter if desired, cook the greens until they are wilted, about half a minute. Season to taste with salt and freshly ground black pepper. Remove to a warm plate.

2 In the same skillet, bring the vermouth and broth to a simmer. Add the sole fillets and poach gently until they are barely opaque, about two minutes. (If the fillets are very small, fold them crosswise so that they are easier to handle and do not flake apart.) Remove the fillets from the liquid and keep them warm in a foil tent in the oven.

3 Unless you are using the poaching liquid in the sauce, pour it away and return the skillet to the heat. Melt the half cup of butter. Add the peppercorns, tarragon and lemon juice. Boil hard for about one minute, until the sauce is thickened and creamy.

4 If you are using the poaching liquid instead of butter for the sauce, add the peppercorns, tarragon and lemon juice. Boil until reduced by half.

5 Make a bed of the cooked greens on each of four plates. Place a fillet on the greens and pour the sauce over. Garnish with a sprig of fresh tarragon and a twist of lemon. Serve with boiled new potatoes dotted with butter and a sprinkling of fines herbes.

He ordered himself a dozen oysters; but, suddenly remembering that the month contained no "r", changed them to a fried sole.

— John Galsworthy
The White Monkey

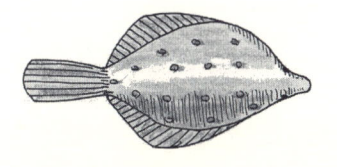

TWENTY-EIGHT BOTTLES AROUND THE BAY

If you are allergic to dairy products, use a non-dairy whipped topping in place of the crème fraîche.

PEPPERED STRAWBERRIES AND CRÈME FRAÎCHE

1 pint (18–20) whole strawberries

About 3/4 cup crème fraîche

Black pepper

1/2 bottle Gewürztraminer Auslese or Riesling Spätlese, well chilled

1 Wash the strawberries and allow them to dry on a paper towel, leaving the green stems intact.

2 Choose four of the nicest berries. Cut them into thin slices from the base to the top, not quite all the way through, and spread the slices out in a fan shape.

3 Coarsely grind a generous amount of black pepper onto each of four dessert plates. Place a dollop of the crème fraîche in the center of each plate, and ring it with whole berries. Place one of the fanned berries on top of the crème fraîche.

4 Serve the berry plates with a glass of the wine. To eat this dish, roll each berry in the pepper, then dip it in the crème fraîche. Follow every bite with a mouthful of wine — a truly ambrosial combination.

TIPS:

The wine is an integral part of this dish. As a substitute, try Asti Spumante or one of the many sweet North American sparkling wines.

If you haven't any crème fraîche, use crème Gervaise, which can be made in moments.

If fresh strawberries aren't available, use frozen (unsweetened) berries. Thaw and drain well and fold them gently into the crème fraîche or crème Gervaise. Serve on dessert plates as before, with the pepper and wine.

This dish also makes an excellent appetizer, especially before roast meat.

As Dr. Boteler said of strawberries:
"Doubtless God could have made a better berry, but doubtless God never did."

— Izaak Walton
The Compleat Angler

MENU TWO

Cardamom-Scented Apple Soup

Asparagus Spears with Egg Mousse and Caviar

Grilled Salmon with Fresh Herb Salsa

Spiced Banana and Rum Crêpes

A delicate soup, with hints of exotic flavors — keep a light hand with the curry powder.

CARDAMOM-SCENTED APPLE SOUP

1 medium leek, white and tender green part only, roughly chopped

3 Granny Smith apples, or other tart cooking apples, peeled, cored, and chopped

1 teaspoon grated or sliced fresh ginger

1 tablespoon butter

1/2–1 teaspoon curry powder

1 teaspoon ground cardamom

1 10-ounce can condensed chicken broth

1/2 cup coconut milk or 10% cream (optional)

1 In a medium heavy saucepan over moderate heat, cook the leeks, apples and ginger gently in the butter until softened, about five minutes. Add the curry powder and cardamom and cook another few seconds, stirring. Add the chicken stock and simmer until the apples are tender, about ten minutes in total.

2 Purée the soup and return it to the pot. Add the coconut milk or cream and reheat gently. Season to taste with salt and freshly ground black pepper.

3 Garnish with a dollop of sour cream, chopped chives or green onions.

TIPS:
The soup may be prepared a day or two ahead, or frozen (without the milk or cream). Reheat gently. It is also excellent cold, in which case you may wish to increase the amount of curry powder and cardamom, since chilling mutes the flavor of spices.

An ordinary yellow cooking onion will do in place of the leek, although the flavor of the soup will not be as delicate. You can turn this into a full-blown curried apple soup, increasing the amount of curry powder to whatever your palate can stand, in which case it makes a warming main dish for a quick luncheon or supper. Serve it with white rice or pita bread on the side.

*Man may live without love — what is passion but pining?
But where is the man who can live without dining?*

*We may live without friends, we may live without books,
But civilized men cannot live without cooks.*

— Owen Meredith
Lucile

Twenty-Eight Bottles Around the Bay

The egg mousse is nice on its own, without the asparagus, served in sorbet dishes.

If you are allergic to dairy products, purée a tin of flaked white tuna with a little olive oil, lemon juice and freshly cracked black pepper to serve with the asparagus instead of the mousse.

ASPARAGUS SPEARS WITH EGG MOUSSE AND CAVIAR

12 asparagus spears, trimmed to 4-inch lengths

4 hard-cooked eggs, peeled and chopped

1 shallot, minced

2 tablespoons mayonnaise

3 tablespoons sour cream or plain yogurt

Juice of half a lemon

Dash cayenne

1 small jar red or black caviar (optional)

TIPS:

If possible, prepare the mousse a day or two ahead to blend the flavors.

As a garnish, in place of the caviar, use finely chopped green onions or chives, chopped green or black olives, crumbled bacon, chopped capers, or pimiento.

If you would like a really smooth mousse, increase the sour cream by a tablespoon or two and purée the egg mixture.

If you don't have time to hard-cook the eggs, use pickled eggs, chopped very finely or pressed through a sieve.

There is always a best way of doing everything, if it be to boil an egg. Manners are the happy ways of doing things.

— Emerson
Conduct of Life

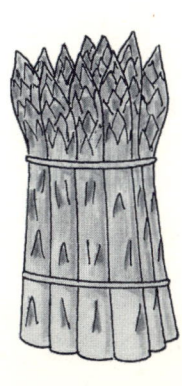

1 Cook the asparagus in boiling salted water until crisp-tender, about three minutes. Drain and chill.

2 In a small bowl, mix the eggs and shallot with the mayonnaise, sour cream and lemon juice. Season with salt and cayenne.

3 Fan three asparagus spears on each of four salad plates. Place a quarter of the mousse at the base of the spears. Garnish with caviar.

The herb salsa goes well with any grilled or broiled fish — try tuna or swordfish steaks — or grilled chicken. A great summer barbecue dish.

GRILLED SALMON WITH FRESH HERB SALSA

- 2 tomatoes, diced
- 1 cup diced English cucumber
- 2 green onions, chopped
- 1/4 cup combination of chopped fresh basil and dill
- 1/4 cup olive oil
- Juice of 1 lemon
- 1 teaspoon sugar
- 4 salmon steaks, 3/4–1 inch thick
- Olive oil

1 In a small, deep bowl, combine tomatoes, cucumber, onions, herbs, olive oil, lemon juice and sugar. Season to taste with salt and freshly ground black pepper. Set aside.

2 Rub the salmon with olive oil. Grill or broil the steaks until lightly charred, about four minutes. Turn and cook until opaque in the center, four to five minutes. Arrange steaks on a warm platter, with the rice heaped in the center and sprigs of fresh herbs, parsley and lemon wedges in between. Serve the salsa in a separate bowl.

BASMATI RICE: Rinse one cup basmati rice in several changes of cold water. In a medium heavy saucepan over high heat, bring to a boil two cups water, rice, and one teaspoon salt. Cover and reduce heat to minimum. Cook until all water is absorbed, about twenty-five minutes. Fluff and allow to stand a few minutes before serving.

Poisson sans boisson est poison.

— French Proverb

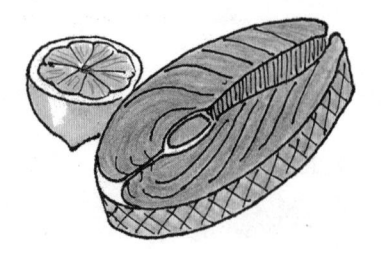

Crêpes are simple to make and freeze well; most grocery stores also carry them ready-made.

SPICED BANANA AND RUM CRÊPES

4 crêpes

4 bananas, peeled and split or sliced (toss in a little lemon juice to keep them from browning)

Butter (optional)

Juice and zest of 1 orange

Cornstarch

1/2 cup dark rum

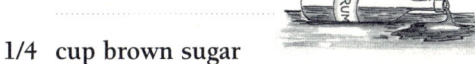

1/4 cup brown sugar

1/2 teaspoon allspice

1 In a medium skillet, in hot butter, sauté the bananas to a light golden brown. If you do not wish to use butter, broil the bananas until sizzling. Set aside.

2 In a small saucepan, combine the orange juice and zest with enough cornstarch to make a paste. Whisk in the rum, sugar, and allspice. Cook over medium heat until thickened.

3 On each of four warmed plates, fill a crêpe with one quarter of the banana slices. Spoon on the hot sauce. Roll up the crêpe. Garnish with a twist of orange.

TIPS:
The crêpes may be made well ahead of time and frozen. The rum sauce may be made several days ahead; reheat it while you sauté the bananas, thinning if necessary with a little more rum.

Virtually any fruit, or combination of fruits, fresh, frozen (thawed and drained), or canned, will work well. Combinations of tropical fruits are especially nice with the rum sauce.

If you like, serve the fruit in the sauce without the crêpes. Pour on a little extra rum and flame it at the table. Top with whipped cream, non-dairy topping, crème fraîche, or ice cream.

1655: Rum from Jamaica is introduced into the Royal Navy to replace beer, which goes sour after a few weeks at sea.

1731: Half a pint of rum in two equal tots becomes the official daily ration for all hands in the British Royal Navy.

MENU THREE

Seafood Coquilles

Chilled Avocado Soup

Medallions of Pork Tenderloin with Calvados

Grapes Gervaise

If you have allergies or don't like seafood, make these coquilles with the mushrooms, brandy, and cheese.

SEAFOOD COQUILLES

1/4 pound mushrooms (about 12 small), sliced

1/4 pound small cooked shrimp (fresh, frozen, or canned)

1/4 pound whole bay scallops

1/4 cup brandy

1 cup freshly shaved Parmesan cheese

TIPS:
Any combination of cooked seafood will work; try lobster or crab meat (well-drained).

The shells may be prepared several hours ahead to this point* and refrigerated until you are ready to cook them.

Give strong drink unto him that is ready to perish, and wine unto those that be of heavy hearts.

Proverbs 31:6

1 In a heavy skillet over moderate heat, sauté the mushrooms in hot butter until golden, about five minutes.

2 Add the scallops and cook until they are barely opaque, about thirty seconds, stirring constantly. Remove from heat. Add the shrimp and brandy. Stir well.

3 Divide the mixture between four scallop shells. Top each with a thick layer of Parmesan cheese and a pat of butter.*

4 Broil until the cheese is golden and bubbling, about five minutes. Garnish with a lemon wedge and sprig of parsley.

Twenty-Eight Bottles Around the Bay   23

CHILLED AVOCADO SOUP

1 ripe avocado

1 10-ounce can condensed chicken broth

1 cup milk or 10% cream

2 shallots, chopped or minced

Juice and grated zest of 1 lime

1 teaspoon ground coriander seed

Dash cayenne

1. Halve the avocado, remove the pit, and scoop out the flesh. Purée with the remaining ingredients until smooth, reserving a little of the zest for garnish. Season with salt and cayenne. Divide the soup among four bowls. Chill for at least fifteen minutes, or up to several hours. Garnish with the reserved lime zest.

TIPS:
Avocado discolors quickly once exposed to the air. Press plastic wrap onto the surface of the soup in order to prevent this or leave the soup in the blender to chill, covering the surface with a thin layer of mayonnaise, which can be stirred in before serving.

In prudent anticipation of your mood I have ventured to dream up and prepare a first course calculated to calm nerves, elevate minds and raise spirits.

— Johannes Mario Simmel
It Can't Always Be Caviar

Calvados is distilled from the apples of Normandy, a golden, distinctively sharp fruity spirit. If necessary, you can use ordinary brandy instead, and add half a cup of dry apple cider.

MEDALLIONS OF PORK TENDERLOIN WITH CALVADOS

4 Golden Delicious apples, cored, cut into thick slices

2 tablespoons brown sugar

Butter (optional)

1 pound pork tenderloin, cut in 1-inch slices, pounded to 1/4-inch thickness

3–4 shallots, coarsely chopped

1 tablespoon fresh thyme leaves

1/2 cup Calvados

1/2 cup 35% cream (optional)

1 In a large heavy skillet over medium-high heat, sauté the apple slices in hot butter and sugar until golden, about two minutes per side. Or toss the apples with the sugar and broil, being careful not to burn the sugar. Set aside.

2 Season the pork with salt and pepper. In a large heavy skillet over moderate heat, sauté pork slices in hot butter until barely cooked through, about two minutes per side. Keep warm in a foil tent in the oven.

3 In the same skillet, adding more butter if necessary, sauté the shallots with the thyme. Add a quarter cup Calvados and reduce to a glaze, scraping up any brown bits. Add the remaining Calvados and cream. Boil until slightly thickened. Season to taste with salt and freshly ground black pepper.

4 Divide the pork among four warmed plates. Spoon the sauce over the pork. Top with apple slices. Garnish with sprigs of thyme. Serve with a chewy pain de campagne — try a fresh crusty rye bread — and a bowl of plain salad greens.

Stay me with flagons, comfort me with apples: for I am sick of love.

— Song of Solomon

TWENTY-EIGHT BOTTLES AROUND THE BAY 25

Crème Gervaise is a brandy-flavored thick sauce which is not meant to be sweet. In Europe, it is made with a mild, unripened cheese known as farmers' cheese. Softened cream cheese is a reasonable substitute, as is — for the truly health-conscious — cottage or ricotta cheese that has been blended to a smooth consistency. If necessary, substitute a non-dairy whipped topping for the cream, but don't forget the brandy.

GRAPES GERVAISE

About 2 cups green, red, or mixed seedless grapes, stems removed

1 3-ounce package cream cheese, softened

1/2 cup thick sour cream

2 ounces brandy or kirsch

1. Divide the grapes among four chilled sorbet glasses or champagne flutes.

2. Sprinkle some of the brandy or kirsch over the grapes.

3. Beat the cream cheese until it is smooth. Stir in the sour cream and remaining brandy. Chill until needed.

4. Spoon the cream over the grapes. Garnish with fresh mint leaves, lemon zest, a sprinkling of Demerara sugar, or a chocolate-coated after-dinner mint.

TIPS:
The crème Gervaise is particularly good with peaches and pears, or with hot mixed fruits. The grapes served with Gervaise cream also make a good appetizer or a side dish for a light luncheon, especially with chicken.

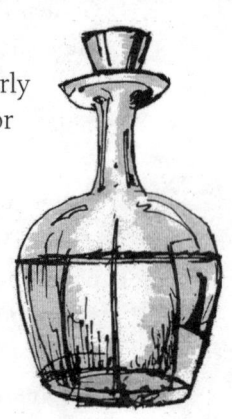

ABLIGURITION. Extravagance in cooking and serving. E.g. "So wise of you to have chosen Mabel, Reginald. Abligurition is such a comforting thing in a fiancée."

— Peter Bowler
The Superior Person's Second Book of Weird and Wondrous Words

MENU FOUR

Spring Green Soup

⚓

Tomato Flowers with Stilton

⚓

Veal in Mushroom and Shallot Cream

⚓

Pots-de-Crème with Cointreau

The crème fraîche in this soup is important, as it smooths out the flavor of the greens and is highly decorative. If you do not wish to use any cream, choose milder greens such as regular leaf lettuce and spinach and use chicken stock instead of beef. The soup is excellent chilled.

SPRING GREEN SOUP

- 1 large onion, finely chopped
- 2 cups packed salad greens (such as lettuce, beet, Swiss chard, dandelion or radish greens, sorrel, or spinach), finely chopped
- Butter
- 1 tablespoon herbed flour
- 1 10-ounce can condensed beef consommé
- 1 tablespoon chopped fresh tarragon, or 1 teaspoon dried
- 1/2 cup crème fraîche (optional)

1 In a medium heavy saucepan over moderate heat, sauté the onion in hot butter until tender, about five minutes. Add the greens and cook until wilted, about two minutes. Sprinkle on the flour and cook a few seconds, until it foams. Whisk in the consommé and one can of water. Bring the soup to a boil, whisking constantly; simmer five to ten minutes to blend the flavors.

2 Remove the pot from the stove. Stir in the tarragon and half of the crème fraîche. Season to taste with salt and freshly ground black pepper.

3 Ladle the soup into four hot bowls. Swirl a little more of the crème fraîche through each serving to produce a marbled effect.

TIPS:
The soup may be made up to two days ahead, or frozen for longer storage. Add the crème fraîche after reheating. Frozen or canned spinach may be used in place of fresh greens. Add a handful of finely chopped fresh parsley, which will improve the color, and cook only until the soup is heated through.

Sour cream or 35% cream may be used in place of the crème fraîche. Don't use regular milk, as it is likely to curdle with the acidity of the greens.

The richness or quality of a soup depends much more upon the art and skill of the cook than upon the sum laid out in the market.

— Count Rumford

TOMATO FLOWERS WITH STILTON

1/4 cup balsamic vinegar

1/4 cup olive oil

1/4 cup chopped fresh basil

4 firm, ripe tomatoes

4 ounces Stilton, crumbled

1 In a small bowl, briefly stir the vinegar, olive oil and basil. Season to taste with salt and freshly ground black pepper.

2 Cut each tomato into a flower by slicing it from the top into eight wedges, not quite all the way through. Spread the wedges gently out to form petals of the flower.

3 Place one tomato in the center of each of four salad plates. Spoon the vinaigrette over each tomato, using all of it.

4 Crumble a quarter of the Stilton into the center of each tomato flower.

5 Garnish with freshly ground black pepper and finely chopped chives or green onions.

TIPS:
Do not refrigerate the tomatoes, as this destroys their flavor.

If fresh basil is not available, use finely chopped fresh parsley instead, mixed with a tablespoon of dried basil leaves.

Instead of Stilton, try any blue-veined cheese, feta, mild mozarella, or shavings of Parmesan. If you prefer to do without cheese, sprinkle the center of each tomato flower with finely chopped Spanish onion, or use a spoonful of basil pesto.

A smell of basil is good for the heart and head — cureth the infirmities of the heart, taketh away sorrowfulness which cometh of melancholia and maketh a man merry and glad.

— John Gerard

Instead of white veal, use turkey breast scallopini, boneless pork cutlets, or skinless, boneless chicken breasts. Pork or chicken must be pounded well, so that it cooks quickly and evenly.

VEAL IN MUSHROOM AND SHALLOT CREAM

4 pieces white veal scallopini

Flour

Butter

1/2 pound baby mushroom caps

4–6 shallots, chopped

1 cup 18% cream

1 cup dry white vermouth

1 Pound the veal lightly. Season well with salt and freshly ground black pepper. Dredge with flour, shaking off the excess. In a large heavy skillet over medium-high heat, sauté the veal in hot butter until just cooked through, about thirty seconds per side. Do not overcook. Keep the veal warm in a foil tent in the oven.

2 In the same skillet, adding more butter if necessary, sauté the mushrooms until golden, about five minutes. Add the shallots; cook one minute. Add the cream and vermouth; boil down to a thick sauce consistency, about three minutes. Season with salt and freshly ground black pepper.

3 Place a piece of veal on each of four warmed plates. Pour the sauce over the veal. Garnish with a few capers and finely chopped parsley.

4 Serve with brown rice and snow peas or French-cut green beans.

TIPS:

Do not use regular red veal; it is not tender or delicate enough in flavor for this dish.

Instead of the cream, you can use a can of Danish thick cream or, in a pinch, evaporated milk.

*When I make a feast
I would my guests should praise it, not the cooks.*
　　　　　　　　— Sir John Harington
　　　　Of Writers Who Carp at Other Men's Books

POTS-DE-CRÈME WITH COINTREAU

- 8 squares semisweet or bittersweet chocolate
- 1/4 cup strong black coffee
- 1 tablespoon butter
- 1 tablespoon Cointreau
- 4 large eggs, separated

1 In a small heavy saucepan over low heat, melt the chocolate with the coffee, stirring continually until smooth. Remove from heat. Stir in the butter and Cointreau. Cool slightly. Beat in the egg yolks.

2 In a deep bowl, beat the egg whites until stiff. Fold the whites into the chocolate mixture. Spoon the mixture into four demitasses or small glasses. Garnish with grated orange zest.

TIPS:
The pots-de-crème may be served immediately, slightly warm, or refrigerated several hours or overnight.

Any orange-flavored liqueur will work, or try Drambuie, Amaretto, or any other liqueur that marries well with chocolate.

When considered in the context of the senses art and cuisine are closely linked — they are both an expression of the senses designed to be shared, experienced and appreciated by others.

— Alain Ducasse
Cézanne and the Provençal Table

MENU FIVE

Clear Leek Soup

❦

Smoked Salmon with Black Pepper Crème Fraîche

❦

Rack of Lamb with Mustard and Rosemary Pesto

❦

Syllabub

We rarely see the leek on its own, which is a shame, as it has an appealing, delicate flavor and texture. This is a clear, appetite-sparking broth which the French call soupe vite, or "fast soup."

CLEAR LEEK SOUP

1 medium potato, peeled and coarsely grated

2–3 medium leeks, white and tender green part, cut in half lengthwise and finely sliced

3 cups water

4 slices French baguette

1–2 tablespoons olive oil

1. Place the potato, leeks and water in a medium saucepan. Over high heat, bring to a boil. Simmer until the vegetables are very tender, about ten minutes. Season to taste with salt and freshly ground black pepper.

2. Place a slice of bread in the bottom of each of four warm soup bowls. Drizzle on some of the olive oil. Ladle the simmering broth over the bread.

TIPS:

In place of the potato, try half a cup of parboiled white rice, couscous, or tiny pasta shells.

For a more substantial soup, replace the water with chicken broth and top each slice of bread with shredded Swiss Emmenthal or Gruyère cheese. If you prefer, broil the bread and cheese and serve it on the side, or float it on top of the soup to produce a very light version of French onion soup.

Good cooking is an art which is easily acquired.... A recipe is not as precise as a chemical formula, since ingredients vary slightly, as do cooking utensils and stoves. But a little difference is sometimes refreshing, and so it will not matter if there is a slight change in the finished product.

— The Fanny Farmer Cookbook (1896)

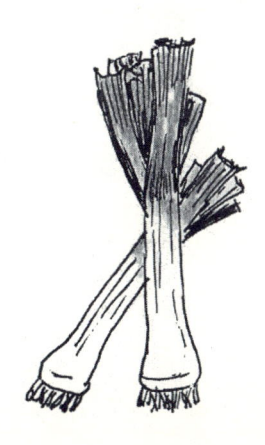

If you don't like fish, try the crème fraîche with sliced avocado (sprinkle lemon juice over the avocado to prevent discoloration) or thinly sliced prosciutto.

SMOKED SALMON WITH BLACK PEPPER CRÈME FRAÎCHE

- 8 thin slices smoked salmon
- 1/2 cup crème fraîche
- 1 tablespoon coarsely ground black pepper
- 1/4 cup mixed fresh dill and chives, finely chopped
- 3 tablespoons capers

TIPS:
The crème fraîche is good with smoked trout, or any combination of smoked seafood, such as mussels or oysters.

'Tis an ill cook that cannot lick his own fingers.

— Shakespeare
Romeo and Juliet

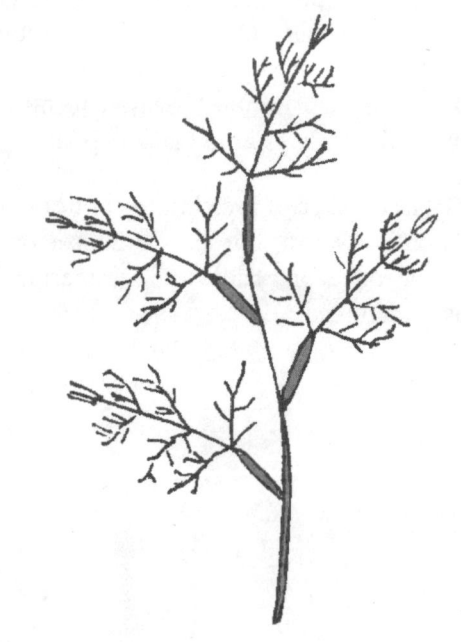

1. Roll each slice of salmon into a cone. Arrange two cones on each of four salad plates, in a V-shape with the narrow ends together. Place a spoonful of crème fraîche at the base of each cone. Sprinkle the salmon with herbs and capers. Garnish with lemon wedges.

RACK OF LAMB WITH MUSTARD AND ROSEMARY PESTO

2 French-trimmed racks of lamb, 7–8 ribs each

Olive oil

2 tablespoons chopped fresh rosemary

1/4 cup chopped fresh parsley

2 large garlic cloves, crushed

2 tablespoons coarse-grained mustard

1/4 cup olive oil

1. Rub the lamb racks with olive oil.

2. In a large heavy oven-proof skillet over high heat, sear the racks until well browned, about three minutes each. Stand the racks in a "guard of honor" position in the skillet, with ribs interlocked.

3. In a small bowl, combine the remaining ingredients. Spread over the meat. Roast at 400°F twelve to fifteen minutes for medium-rare. Cover with foil and allow to stand ten minutes.

4. Cut the racks between the bones and fan on warmed plates. Garnish with a sprig of fresh rosemary.

TIPS:
The racks will go from rare to overdone in a very few minutes. The standing time is vital, as the meat continues to cook, and the juices must be allowed to settle before carving. The lamb may be seared ahead of time and left in the skillet, covered loosely with foil. Put it into the oven when you sit down to your soup.

ROASTED POTATO AND MUSHROOM SALAD: Cut three medium red-skinned potatoes into six wedges each. Thickly slice two or three portobello mushroom caps.

Place the potatoes and mushrooms in separate small bowls. Toss each with enough olive oil to coat and a generous amount of salt and freshly ground black pepper. Roast the potatoes fifteen minutes at 400°F. Add the mushrooms and continue roasting until all are brown and crisp, about ten more minutes.

Toss mixed salad greens with any favorite vinaigrette (try the red wine vinegar dressing used for the crudités in Menu Nine). Divide among four plates. Mound some of the potato and mushroom mixture on each salad.

TIPS:
Use any combination of wild mushrooms. Ordinary white mushrooms are fine but will lack the intensity of flavor. Don't cut them too small as they shrink a lot in the roasting.

Strange to see how a good dinner and feasting reconciles everybody.

— From the diary of Samuel Pepys

TWENTY-EIGHT BOTTLES AROUND THE BAY

The syllabub may be made, if necessary, with a non-dairy whipped topping. Adjust the amount of sugar accordingly.

SYLLABUB

1/4–1/2 cup brandy, or mixed brandy and sherry

1/4 cup sugar

Grated zest and juice of 1 lemon

1 cup 35% cream

1. Place the brandy, sugar, lemon juice and zest in a deep bowl. Stir until the sugar dissolves.

2. Add the cream and beat until thick, about three minutes (it will not form stiff peaks). Spoon into four champagne flutes or sorbet glasses.

3. The syllabub can be served immediately, or chilled for several hours, in which case it will have a firmer, mousse-like texture.

4. Garnish with mint leaves or rosemary, or a slice of lemon.

TIPS:
The quantities given here make a tart, lemony, richly alcoholic dessert. If you generally prefer sweeter desserts, increase the sugar to half a cup. It would not hurt, for four people, to halve the recipe, especially if you serve the syllabub in chocolate cups.

I closed my eyes and heard only a breeze that ventured, and retreated, and returned shyly to stay, and I was drunk with pleasure; in an ecstasy of happiness.

— Nigel Buxton
Walking in Wine Country

36   TWENTY-EIGHT BOTTLES AROUND THE BAY

MENU SIX

Garlic Soup

❦

Chèvre-Stuffed Pears with Cumin Sauce

❦

Savory Crêpes with Herb-Seasoned Filling

❦

Raspberry Fool

Don't let the name of this soup scare you. The garlic, simmered in this way, becomes sweet and mild, with none of the after effects you expect from raw or quickly cooked garlic. Garlic soup is highly valued by French cooks for its health benefits, as it is supposed to lower blood pressure and cleanse the liver.

GARLIC SOUP

1   10-ounce can condensed chicken broth

6–8 large garlic cloves, peeled

1   sprig fresh thyme

1   bay leaf

4   slices French baguette, buttered and toasted

4   ounces freshly shaved Gruyère or Emmenthal cheese

1 In a medium saucepan over high heat, bring the chicken broth, one full can of water, garlic cloves, thyme and bay leaf to a boil. Reduce heat and simmer until the garlic is tender, about fifteen minutes.

2 Remove the thyme and bay leaf. Mash the garlic to a paste with the back of a spoon and stir it back into the soup.

3 Return the soup to heat. Season to taste with salt and freshly ground black pepper.

4 Place one of the toast slices in the bottom of each of four warmed soup bowls. Sprinkle with cheese. Pour the soup over the cheese. Garnish with a sprinkling of fines herbes.

TIPS:
To speed the cooking, put the garlic cloves through a press before adding to the soup.

Chicken stock is not essential to this soup; you may use water instead, adding a splash of olive oil and four or five sage leaves, if you have them.

Because this soup is so light and perks up the taste buds, it makes an excellent appetizer. In the south of France, when the howling wind known as the mistral blows in, this soup is made more comfortably substantial with eggs. Crack four eggs into the simmering broth after you have mashed the garlic, allowing them to poach lightly. Place the toast as before in each bowl and top with an egg and the cheese. Then pour in the broth. A great quick lunch or supper dish for tired and hungry sailors, too!

*Wel loved he garleek, oynons, and eek lekes,
And for to drynken strong wyn, reed as blood.*

— Chaucer
The Canterbury Tales

Cumin has a strong, earthy taste with citrus overtones, which both enhances the flavor of the goat cheese and complements the sweetness of the pears.

CHÈVRE-STUFFED PEARS WITH CUMIN SAUCE

2 large firm ripe pears, halved and cored

1/2 cup soft mild goat cheese

Dash cayenne

1/4 cup sour cream

1/4 cup mayonnaise

1 tablespoon fresh lemon juice

1 tablespoon cumin

TIPS:
The stuffed pears may be wrapped tightly and chilled several hours or overnight. Instead of chèvre, try finely grated sharp white Cheddar cheese. For a lighter dressing, use plain yogurt in place of the mayonnaise.

The stuffed pears also make a nice dessert.

All that the curious palate could wish.
— T. H. Aldrich
When the Sultan Goes to Ispahan

1 Brush the cut sides of the pears with lemon juice or white vinegar.

2 In a small bowl, beat the cheese with the cayenne. Season to taste with salt and freshly ground black pepper. Pack the cheese into the pear cavities. In a small measuring cup, blend the sour cream, mayonnaise, lemon juice and cumin.

3 With a knife dipped in hot water, cut each pear half into two or three wedges. Spoon some of the dressing onto each of four salad plates and fan the pear wedges around the dressing. Garnish with a sprinkling of fines herbes.

This easy, elegant meal can be prepared in moments from leftovers. Crêpes are simple to make and freeze well; most grocery stores also carry them ready-made.

SAVORY CRÊPES WITH HERB-SEASONED FILLING

1/2 pound mushrooms, any variety, chopped

2 tablespoons butter

2 tablespoons herbed flour

About 1 cup hot milk

1 cup frozen French-sliced green beans, defrosted

1 tomato, chopped

1 tablespoon capers

1 pound (about 2 cups) sliced cooked chicken, lamb, pork, veal — whatever you have on hand

4 crêpes

Freshly grated cheese (Emmenthal, Gruyère, or Cheddar)

1 In a large heavy skillet over moderate heat, in hot butter, cook the mushrooms until golden, about five minutes. Stir in the flour. Add the milk, stirring constantly, until the sauce is smooth and thick.

2 Stir in the beans, tomato, capers and meat. Season with salt and freshly ground black pepper. Fill the crêpes with the mixture and roll up. Top with a little cheese. Bake on a greased baking sheet at 375°F until the cheese is melted and the filling is hot, ten to fifteen minutes. Garnish with a sprig of any fresh herb.

3 Serve an appropriate relish on the side — mango chutney with chicken, red currant preserve with lamb, applesauce with pork.

TIPS:

If you haven't any leftover cooked meat on hand, brown a pound of ground meat in another heavy skillet while the mushrooms are cooking. For a meatless dinner, add a cup of grated cheese to the sauce and substitute two cups of any combination of frozen (defrosted) vegetables for the meat.

Is thy cruse of comfort wasting?
Rise and share it with another,
And through all the years of famine
It shall serve thee and thy brother;
Love divine will fill thy storehouse,
Or thy handful still renew
Scanty fare for one will often
Make a royal feast for two.

— Mrs. E. R. Charles

A fool, in the culinary sense, is a fruit purée folded into whipped cream. Some like to substitute custard for part of the cream; this is especially nice if you are using a tart fruit such as gooseberries. If you are allergic to dairy products, a fool may be made successfully using a non-dairy whipped topping, in which case you can do without any added sugar and may even want to use a sprinkling of lemon juice to cut through the sweetness. Whatever combination of fruits and cream or custard you use, a dash of kirsch or another suitable liqueur is always a tasteful addition.

RASPBERRY FOOL

3 cups fresh raspberries or frozen unsweetened raspberries, thawed and well drained

1 cup 35% cream, well chilled

1/4 cup icing sugar

1 teaspoon almond extract

1 Purée two cups of the berries. Strain through a sieve only if the pips bother you. Reserve half a cup of the purée.

2 In a deep bowl, beat the remaining purée with the cream, sugar and almond extract, until firm peaks form. Fold the remaining cup of berries into the cream mixture. Spoon into four sorbet glasses or champagne flutes. Drizzle with the reserved purée.

3 Garnish with a few fresh berries, mint leaves, lemon zest, or sprigs of fresh herbs. Dust with icing sugar.

TIPS:
Instead of raspberries, use fresh or frozen strawberries, blueberries, or cherries.
If you have a sweet tooth, you may wish to add a little icing sugar to the reserved purée.

The fool may be prepared several hours ahead; only be sure, if you are using frozen fruit, that it is very well drained.

If possible, chill the mixing bowl, beaters and glasses before beginning so that the cream will whip into firm peaks and remain stiff. Should it flop on you, either because the cream is not cold enough or there is too much liquid in the fruit, put it in the freezer for half an hour or so to firm it up; stir gently before serving.

Eating is not merely a material pleasure. Eating well gives a spectacular joy to life and contributes immensely to goodwill and happy companionship. It is of great importance to the morale.

— Elsa Schiaparelli (1890–1973),
Italian fashion designer

TWENTY-EIGHT BOTTLES AROUND THE BAY

MENU SEVEN

Broiled Roquefort

Chilled Herb and Parsley Soup

Champagne Chicken

Pound Cake Croustades with Brandied Fruit

BROILED ROQUEFORT

- 2 thick slices stale white sandwich bread, buttered, crusts removed

- 1/4 pound Roquefort, or other good blue cheese, crumbled

- 4 slices bacon, crisply cooked and crumbled

- 4 moist dates, finely chopped

1 Cut each bread slice diagonally into four triangles. Bake in a 400°F oven ten minutes or until golden.

2 In a medium bowl, beat together the cheese, bacon and dates. Spread some of the mixture on each bread triangle, using all of it.*

3 Broil the toasts until the cheese mixture is hot and bubbly, five to ten minutes. Place two triangles, slightly overlapping, on each of four plates. Garnish with whole green onions or a few chive stems.

*The toasts may be prepared ahead to this point and frozen. Heat in a 425°F oven about ten to fifteen minutes.

TIPS:
Broiled Roquefort is also nice as a dessert, served with fresh fruit.

Many's the long night I've dreamed of cheese — toasted mostly.

— Robert Louis Stevenson
Treasure Island

This soup makes a refreshing course in between the hot cheese and main dish, as a change from salad, but may also be served hot. If you do serve it hot, omit the yogurt, and be sure not to let the soup cook any longer than necessary for it to heat through or you will lose that fresh, appetite-stimulating herb flavor. Stir in a little crème fraîche or sour cream just before serving.

CHILLED HERB AND PARSLEY SOUP

1 medium onion, roughly chopped

1 medium potato, peeled and coarsely grated

1 cup water

1 cup dry white vermouth

1 bunch fresh parsley, coarse stems removed, roughly chopped

3–4 tablespoons chopped fresh herbs (such as thyme, savory, chervil, and tarragon)

1/2 cup plain yogurt or crème fraîche

1 In a medium saucepan over moderate heat, simmer the potato and onion in the water and vermouth until they begin to soften, about five minutes. Add the parsley and simmer until the vegetables are very tender, another five minutes or so. Remove from heat.* Add the herbs and allow the soup to cool slightly.

2 Purée the soup. Pour it into a bowl or covered dish. Stir in the yogurt. Season to taste with salt and freshly ground black pepper. Chill at least half an hour, up to several hours, or overnight.

3 Check for seasoning. Ladle into chilled soup bowls or glass dessert dishes. Garnish with a dollop of yogurt and a sprinkling of any chopped fresh herbs, parsley, or chives.

*This soup can also be turned into a jellied salad. Prepare it to this point. Stir in one envelope (one tablespoon) gelatine and the juice of one lemon. Purée the mixture, then stir in the chopped herbs. Divide the purée between four small oiled ramekins. Chill until set, at least two hours or overnight. Sprinkle four salad plates with fines herbes. Unmold one jellied salad onto the center of each plate. Top with a spoonful of yogurt, sour cream, or crème fraîche.

TIPS:
Use the parsley alone if no fresh herbs are available; dried herbs will not do for this dish. Italian flat-leaf parsley has a better flavor than the familiar curly parsley. To chill the soup quickly, place in a metal bowl in the freezer.

In imperial Rome, parsley was fashioned into crowns for banquet guests. This, the host hoped, would prevent drunkenness and raucousness at the table.

— Day and Stuckey
The Spice Cookbook

For this dish, I often use the breasts from a couple of whole roast chickens, making soup and stock out of the rest. This cuts down on the amount of butter, and the meat is beautifully moist and tender. You may also poach the chicken in a light broth.

CHAMPAGNE CHICKEN

4	skinless boneless chicken breast halves
	Cornstarch or potato flour
	Butter
1/2	bottle champagne or dry sparkling white wine
1	10-ounce can condensed chicken broth
1/4	cup butter

1 Dredge the chicken breasts with cornstarch. In a heavy skillet over medium-high heat, sauté the chicken in hot butter until barely cooked, about three minutes per side. Do not overcook. Keep warm in a foil tent in the oven.

2 Add the broth and champagne to the skillet. Boil until reduced to about one cup, about five minutes. Remove from heat. Swirl in the quarter cup of butter until it is melted and the sauce is smooth. Rewarm over gentle heat.

3 Slice each chicken breast across the grain, not quite all the way through, and fan slightly. Arrange one breast on each of four warmed plates. Spoon the sauce over the chicken.

4 Garnish with thin strips of lemon and a sprig of fresh rosemary.

ROSEMARY POTATOES: In a medium saucepan, in salted water, boil twelve new potatoes in their skins until tender. Drain. Toss with a little unsalted butter, sea salt and a tablespoon of chopped fresh rosemary.

SWEET PEPPER MEDLEY: Halve and seed one red and one yellow or green sweet pepper. Cut each half into six pieces. In a heavy medium skillet over high heat, in a little olive oil, sear the vegetables until they are slightly blackened and blistering, about five minutes. Season with a generous pinch of sea salt.

TIPS:
The potatoes and peppers may be prepared a day ahead. Reheat them gently.

The chicken, potatoes and peppers are all delicious served at room temperature or chilled. Just toss the potatoes with olive oil instead of butter.

No poems can please for long or live that are written by water-drinkers.

— Horace
Epistles

TWENTY-EIGHT BOTTLES AROUND THE BAY   45

Croustades are slices of bread or cake, toasted or baked, which are topped with sweet or savory mixtures. In place of pound cake, use sliced muffins, carrot or raisin bread.

POUND CAKE CROUSTADES WITH BRANDIED FRUIT

2 cups chopped fresh or canned fruit (such as peaches, pears, pineapple, kiwis, or grapes)

1/2 cup brandy

About 2 tablespoons sugar (to taste)

2 thick slices pound cake, lightly toasted

Whipped cream, crème fraîche, or vanilla ice cream

1 In a medium non-metallic bowl, mix the fruit with the brandy and sugar. Cover and leave at room temperature for at least an hour, or chill for up to several days, stirring when you think of it.

2 Cut each cake slice in half diagonally. Place a triangle on each of four dessert plates, with a spoonful of the brandied fruit. Top with cream, crème fraîche, or ice cream.

TIPS:
Do not use berries, which bleed color when marinated with sugar.

For a slightly more time-consuming but very pleasing presentation, slice the pound cake about an inch thick and hollow out the center of each slice before toasting. Fill the hollow with whipped cream, crème fraîche, or ice cream. Spoon on the fruit.

*A heavenly paradise is that place
Wherein all pleasant fruits do flow.*

— Thomas Campion
"Cherry-Ripe"

Twenty-Eight Bottles Around the Bay

MENU EIGHT

Sea Scallop Soup

⚓

Zucchini in Olive Oil with Toasted Pine Nuts and Golden Raisins

⚓

Pepper-Crusted Beef Tenderloin in Black Olive Butter

⚓

Peach Chiffon

If you have allergies or don't like seafood, substitute white vermouth for the clam juice, and serve the broth without the scallops.

SEA SCALLOP SOUP

1/2   pound sea scallops, thinly sliced

2   cups strong chicken broth

1/2   cup clam juice or seafood broth

1/2   cup dry white vermouth

1 Divide the sliced scallops among four soup bowls.

2 Pour the broths and vermouth in a medium saucepan and bring to a hard boil. Pour the boiling broth over the scallops — they will be cooked to perfection by the heat of the broth.

3 Garnish the soup with finely chopped green onions or chives.

TIPS:
Bay scallops can be used instead of sea scallops, although the effect is not quite as elegant. Leave bay scallops whole.

Frozen scallops, which may be more readily available, are fine. Thaw and drain well before using. Always be sure to wash scallops thoroughly, as they often have traces of sand, which can ruin a dish.

Come, come, good wine is a good familiar creature if it be well used: exclaim no more against it.

— Shakespeare
Othello

48   TWENTY-EIGHT BOTTLES AROUND THE BAY

This salad was devised for me by a gifted young chef named Sebastian one early summer evening when I stumbled into the stone-walled courtyard of his remote village café in the South of France. After a day of hiking through the garrigue, with the roar of the mistral in my ears and my eyes half blinded by the fierce Provençal sun, I was as giddy as after a day at sea. I thought that the chilled dish which he set before me, mounded high with courgette glistening in golden-green olive oil harvested from the hills below us — speckled with sweet plump raisins, and redolent with the haunting scent of fresh tarragon — was the height of gastronomic pleasure and earthly delight.

ZUCCHINI IN OLIVE OIL WITH TOASTED PINE NUTS AND GOLDEN RAISINS

1–2 baby zucchini, thinly sliced (about 2 cups)

Juice of one lemon

1/4 cup olive oil

1 tablespoon chopped fresh tarragon, or fines herbes

1 tablespoon whole coriander seed

1/2 cup freshly shaved Parmesan cheese

1/4 cup toasted pine nuts

1/4 cup golden raisins

1 In a small bowl, toss the sliced zucchini well with the lemon juice, olive oil, tarragon and coriander seed. Season to taste with salt and freshly ground black pepper.*

2 Divide the zucchini among four salad plates. Sprinkle with the cheese, nuts and raisins.

*The zucchini can be prepared ahead to this point and chilled up to several hours or overnight.

TIPS:
Slivered almonds can be substituted for the pine nuts. Do not use regular raisins in place of golden raisins, as they have quite a different flavor and texture. Diced dried apricots are a fine substitute. Failing that, make the salad without the dried fruit.

This salad makes a delicious base for a main luncheon or light supper dish. Line a bowl first with mixed salad greens, mound the zucchini on the greens, then add strips of smoked ham and turkey.

You may proclaim, good sirs, your fine philosophy.
But till you feed us, right and wrong can wait.

— Bertolt Brecht

Barbecuing the tenderloin and accompanying tomatoes gives them a delicious extra flavor, though they will then require more of your attention during the cooking. For two people only, a smaller tenderloin can be cooked under the broiler in a very few minutes, making this a particularly nice choice for an evening when you'd like a romantic dinner but don't feel you have the time or energy to slave over the stove.

PEPPER-CRUSTED BEEF TENDERLOIN IN BLACK OLIVE BUTTER

1/4	cup butter
1	tablespoon Worcestershire sauce
3/4	cup red wine
5	garlic cloves, crushed
3/4	cup chopped black brine-cured olives
	2-pound beef tenderloin roast
1/4	cup mixed peppercorns, coarsely crushed
	Olive oil

1. In a small heavy saucepan over medium-high heat, melt the butter. Add the red wine, garlic and olives. Cook until bubbly and set aside.

2. Rub the tenderloin with olive oil. Roll in the crushed peppercorns. In a heavy ovenproof skillet over high heat, sear the meat until it is well browned on all sides, about five minutes. Place the skillet in a 350°F oven. Roast the tenderloin until done, about thirty minutes for rare. Cover with foil and allow to stand ten minutes.

3. Bring the sauce to a simmer. Slice the beef and divide it among four warmed plates. Spoon the sauce over the meat. Garnish with a sprinkling of chopped parsley. Serve with cherry tomatoes (see below) and linguine or fettucine.

GRILLED CHERRY TOMATOES: Toss twelve cherry tomatoes with a little olive oil and salt. Broil until they are hot and the skin begins to blacken, about five minutes.

TIPS:
The standing time for the meat is vital to allow the juices to settle. Try to time it so that the roast stands while you have your salad. Grill the tomatoes while you are carving the tenderloin. If you can't get cherry tomatoes, cut large tomatoes in half and grill skin side up.

One can become a cook, but one is born a roaster of meat.

— Anthelme Brillat-Savarin
Physiologie du Goût

Chiffon is a light dessert that goes well after a robust main course. For an exotic twist, purée a ripe mango along with the peaches. The chiffon is also excellent with pears (use Cointreau instead of Amaretto, and lime in place of the lemon). If you are allergic to dairy products, substitute non-dairy whipped topping for the yogurt.

PEACH CHIFFON

- 1 19-ounce can sliced or halved peaches, packed in fruit juice; or 3 fresh ripe peaches, peeled and halved, stones removed and 1 cup white grape juice or white wine

- 1 envelope (1 tablespoon) unflavored gelatine

- Juice and grated zest of 1 lemon

- About 2 tablespoons Amaretto (to taste), or 1 teaspoon almond extract

- 3/4 cup plain yogurt, sour cream, cream or crème fraîche

1 Drain canned fruit well, reserving one cup of the liquid. If you are using fresh peaches, or if the canned fruit is packed in sugar syrup, use white grape juice or wine instead. In a small saucepan, sprinkle the gelatine over the juice or wine. Stir over low heat until the gelatine dissolves. Remove from heat.

2 Purée together the peaches, lemon juice, zest, Amaretto, yogurt and dissolved gelatine until the mixture is smooth and frothy. Pour the purée into sorbet glasses, small ramekins, or chocolate cups. Chill until set, about two hours. Garnish with mint leaves, chopped almonds, lemon zest, or sprigs of fresh thyme.

TIPS:
This recipe makes a light, soft chiffon. For a firmer-textured dessert, decrease the amount of juice or wine (you will need at least a quarter cup to dissolve the gelatine).

For a really fast dessert, make a fruit whip. Beat two egg whites until stiff, then purée together the fruit, lemon juice, zest and Amaretto. Fold the purée gently into the beaten whites. This works best if the fruit is very cold, and it must be served within half an hour or it will separate. I have often made this as an emergency dessert, using a jar of applesauce from the fridge and crème de menthe instead of the Amaretto — beautifully light and refreshing.

The fruit purée also makes a delightful chilled fruit soup, ideal as an elegant starter for a light luncheon or summer dinner. Make as above, omitting the gelatine and blending the reserved juice or wine directly with the fruit.

The smell of the fruit and the wine blew towards them like a promise of all happiness.

— C. S. Lewis
The Voyage of the Dawn Treader

MENU NINE

Crudités with Herbed Dijon Vinaigrette

❧

Braised Beef in Red Wine

❧

Roasted Camembert with Raspberry Coulis and Walnuts

This is a classic French country meal, casual, low cost, and easy to prepare well ahead of time. Crudités — raw vegetables — are familiar to North Americans as hors d'oeuvres served at cocktail parties and buffets. Prepared in this way, they make a colorful, palate-stimulating first course. The quantities given, particularly for the vinaigrette, are only a rough guide. Add any other fresh herbs according to availability and your taste preference.

CRUDITÉS WITH HERBED DIJON VINAIGRETTE

1/4 cup red wine vinegar

3 tablespoons Dijon mustard

1/2 cup olive oil

1 tablespoon chopped fresh basil

1 teaspoon chopped fresh rosemary

1 tablespoon chopped chives or green onions

1 baby zucchini or half an English cucumber, grated or very thinly sliced

1 medium raw beet, peeled and grated

1 carrot, peeled and grated

4 radishes, with some of the green top left on

1 In a small jar with a screw top, shake the dressing ingredients until they are well emulsified. Season to taste with salt and freshly ground black pepper.

2 Place the zucchini, beets, and carrots in separate small bowls. Toss each with enough of the dressing to coat well.

3 Serve the crudités immediately on chilled plates, or cover and chill until needed, up to several hours or overnight.

4 To serve, place a spoonful of the zucchini, beet and carrot on each of four salad plates, with a radish in the center. Serve with a good crusty French stick and any leftover dressing on the side.

TIPS:
With the addition of potatoes in aïoli, these crudités make a delightful warm-weather luncheon or light supper. Boil about twelve new potatoes, or two to three large potatoes, in salted water until tender (peel the potatoes only if the skin is thick). Drain. When they are cool enough to handle, cut the new potatoes in half, or cut the larger potatoes into thick slices. Mix the potatoes gently with enough aïoli to coat. Serve slightly warm, at room temperature, or well-chilled.

*As aromatic plants bestow
No spicy fragrance while they grow;
But crushed or trodden to the ground,
Diffuse their balmy scents around.*

— Oliver Goldsmith
The Captivity

TWENTY-EIGHT BOTTLES AROUND THE BAY

Lamb shanks are also excellent prepared this way — with the addition of a sprig of fresh rosemary.

BRAISED BEEF IN RED WINE

4 ounces salt pork or thick bacon, cubed

2–3 pieces beef shank, bone in

1/2 jar cocktail onions (about 20) or 1 large onion, peeled and sliced

2 carrots, peeled and sliced, or about 12 ready-to-eat mini carrots

5–7 large garlic cloves, peeled

1 tablespoon dried thyme leaves, or a sprig of fresh thyme

1 bay leaf

1 10-ounce can condensed beef consommé

1/2 bottle dry red wine

1/2 cup brandy

2–3 tablespoons tomato paste

1 In a large heavy casserole over medium heat, cook the salt pork or bacon for a minute or two, stirring, until the fat begins to run. Remove the pieces to a plate. Increase heat to high. When the pan is very hot, sear the beef quickly on both sides. Remove from heat.

2 Return the salt pork to the pot. Add the onions, carrots, garlic, thyme, bay leaf, consommé, wine, and brandy. Cover tightly and cook in a 225°F oven for about five hours, until the meat is fork-tender.

3 Stir in enough tomato paste to thicken the gravy. Season to taste with salt, if necessary, and freshly ground black pepper.

4 Serve with more good crusty bread, and, if you like, hot buttered noodles.

TIPS:
Sear the meat quickly over the highest possible heat. It is the brown residue left on the bottom of the pot from the searing that gives the dish its rich color and flavor.

Equally important is the long cooking at a low temperature. Check the surface of the dish after an hour — it should barely move. If it is bubbling, reduce the oven temperature by 25°. You can also cook it overnight, at any temperature between 160 and 180°F. Prepare this dish a day or more ahead; the flavor only improves. It also freezes well.

She looked over his shoulder for vines and olive trees,
Marble, well-governed cities and ships upon wine-dark seas...

— W. H. Auden
The Shield of Achilles

Brie can be used in place of the Camembert.

ROASTED CAMEMBERT WITH RASPBERRY COULIS AND WALNUTS

1 baby Camembert round

1/2 cup chopped walnuts

2 tablespoons butter

1 cup fresh or frozen (thawed and drained) raspberries

Juice of half a lemon

2 tablespoons icing sugar (optional)

1 Place the Camembert round on a greased baking sheet. Roast at 400°F for ten minutes.

2 Meanwhile, in a small heavy sauce pan over medium heat, melt the butter until it is foaming and just beginning to brown. Add the walnuts, stir for a few seconds, and remove from heat.

3 Purée the raspberries with the lemon juice and sugar. Pour the coulis into a small heavy sauce pan and heat gently.

4 To serve, spoon a quarter of the raspberry coulis onto each of four dessert plates. With a knife dipped in hot water, cut the roasted cheese round into four wedges and place one wedge on each plate. Top with the walnut and butter mixture, dividing it evenly among the plates.

TIPS:

If you do not have raspberries, cranberry sauce or melted red currant jelly makes a good substitute (do not add any sugar). Slivered almonds or crushed hazelnuts are delicious alternatives to the walnuts.

If you can find very small Camembert rounds, serve a whole one each for an exceptionally elegant presentation. This also makes a nice first course, or a main course for a light luncheon.

A dessert without cheese is like a beautiful woman with only one eye.

— Anthelme Brillat-Savarin
Physiologie du Goût

MENU TEN

Chick-Pea Soup with Aïoli

Fennel and Orange Salad

Angolotti in Roasted Red Pepper Sauce

Hot Glazed Fruit

This is a classic peasant soup — use almost any vegetables you have on hand, raw (finely chopped), cooked leftovers, or frozen. Make it into a hearty supper dish by increasing the amounts of vegetables relative to the stock. Thicken the soup if you like by making a purée with some of the chick-peas.

CHICK-PEA SOUP WITH AÏOLI

1 10-ounce can condensed chicken stock or beef consommé

1 cup canned chick-peas

1 stalk celery, chopped (leaves, too, if you like)

1 carrot, peeled and chopped

1 leek, white and tender green part only, chopped, or one small onion, chopped.

Other good additions: zucchini, sweet peppers, broccoli, cauliflower or asparagus tips

About 1/2 cup aïoli

About 1 cup shredded Emmenthal or Gruyère cheese (optional)

1 In a medium saucepan, bring the broth and one full can of water to a boil. Add the chick-peas and vegetables and simmer until they are tender, about ten minutes. Season with salt and freshly ground black pepper, remembering that the aïoli will add quite a hot dash of flavoring.

2 Divide the soup among four warmed bowls. Garnish with a handful of chopped parsley. Serve with slices of toasted French baguette or Melba toasts, with the aïoli and cheese on the side.

TIPS:
You can make this soup with water, or part water and part white wine, instead of the broth, but don't serve it without the aïoli — it is not a garnish but an integral part of the soup.

I must add a few words in advocacy of the further adoption in this country of the French practice of using as potage the water in which vegetables generally have been boiled.

— Mattieu Williams

TWENTY-EIGHT BOTTLES AROUND THE BAY 57

This refreshing salad is particularly nice as a light luncheon or supper on a hot summer's day, served with a chunk of Asiago or good aged Parmesan cheese and a loaf of crusty, chewy Calabrese bread.

FENNEL AND ORANGE SALAD

1/4 cup olive oil

Juice of half a lemon

1 teaspoon sharp mustard

1 large fennel bulb

1 seedless orange

2 green onions, or a small bunch of chives, chopped

1 In a small jar with a screw top, shake the oil, lemon juice, and mustard together until well emulsified. Season with salt and freshly ground pepper.

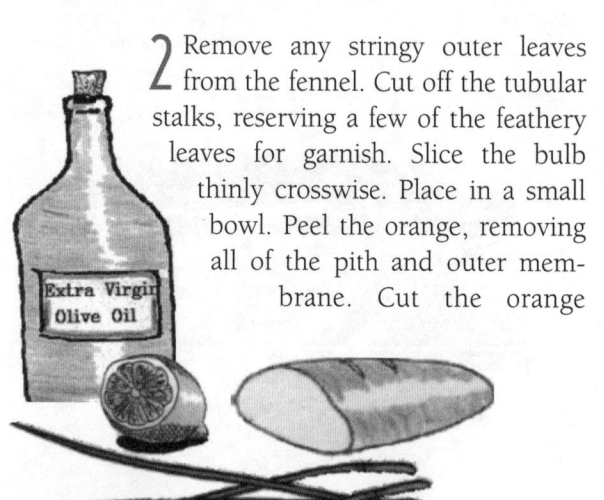

2 Remove any stringy outer leaves from the fennel. Cut off the tubular stalks, reserving a few of the feathery leaves for garnish. Slice the bulb thinly crosswise. Place in a small bowl. Peel the orange, removing all of the pith and outer membrane. Cut the orange crosswise into thin slices. Quarter the slices and add them to the fennel, along with any juice. Add the green onions or chives to the bowl, pour on the dressing and toss gently.

3 Divide the mixture among four salad plates. Garnish with a sprinkling of the reserved leaves, roughly chopped if they are very large.

TIPS:
If you are really pressed for time, use canned mandarin orange segments instead of peeling a fresh orange.

While serving, don't let your guest help you, as that would only cause chaos and confusion, which would be bad for your digestion. Have him stay at the table, and if he's enjoying what he's eating, he won't even notice that you've left him alone for a minute.

— Edouard de Pomiane
French Cooking in 10 Minutes

Agnolotti is a stuffed pasta that is appealing as a main course pasta. Any filled pastas go well with this sauce, especially those stuffed with spinach and cheese. For a nice finishing touch, add a splash of vodka to the sauce just before stirring in the pasta.

AGNOLOTTI IN ROASTED RED PEPPER SAUCE

1/4 cup olive oil

2 large garlic cloves, crushed

2 roasted red bell peppers

1 lb. fresh agnolotti

1–2 cups freshly shaved Parmesan cheese

1. In a large heavy saucepan over moderate heat, cook the garlic in the olive oil until it is beginning to brown, about a minute.

2. Purée the roasted peppers and stir into the olive oil and garlic. Warm the sauce gently over low heat, to smooth and blend the flavors.

3. Meanwhile, cook the agnolotti in boiling salted water until barely tender, about ten minutes. Drain well.

4. Add the pasta to the sauce and stir gently until it is evenly coated. Divide among four very hot pasta bowls. Garnish with the Parmesan cheese and plenty of coarsely ground black pepper.

5. If you feel the need for an accompaniment, serve a big bowl of salad greens tossed with some olive oil and balsamic vinegar.

TIPS:
If necessary, you can pre-cook the agnolotti, but make sure that it is slightly undercooked so that it won't be ruined when you reheat it. Have a pot of water simmering on the stove during the first courses, then plunge the pasta into it briefly while the sauce is heating through. The sauce can be prepared up to several days ahead: refrigerate it in a screw-top jar, with a thin layer of olive oil on top.

He that is of a merry heart hath a continual feast.

— Proverbs 15:15

This fruit is also very good served on pound cake croustades (see Menu Seven), with plain vanilla ice cream as an interesting contrast to the hot fruit.

HOT GLAZED FRUIT

1/4 cup thin-cut orange marmalade

1/4 cup butter

2–3 tablespoons Grand Marnier or other orange liqueur

2 cups mixed sliced fruit (apple wedges, mandarin orange segments, sliced kiwi, pineapple, strawberries, pears, or bananas)

1 cup crème Gervaise, crème fraîche, or whipped cream

TIPS:
Prepare the fruit several hours ahead. Toss with lemon juice and refrigerate.

The sauce can be made in moments, such as when you are making the coffee after the main course.

*You'll have no scandal while you dine,
But honest talk and wholesome wine.*

— Tennyson
"To the Reverend F. D. Morris"

1 In a medium heavy saucepan over moderate heat, melt together the butter and marmalade. Add the liqueur. Cook until hot and bubbly. Add the fruit and heat through gently.

2 Dust four dessert plates with icing sugar. Divide the fruit among the plates. Top with a dollop of crème Gervaise, crème fraîche or whipped cream.

COOKING TIPS

AÏOLI: This pungent garlic mayonnaise is used frequently in French and Italian cooking. To make it, place five crushed garlic cloves, one egg, and the juice of half a lemon in a blender. Process for a few seconds. With the blender on low speed, pour in about one cup of olive oil, in a slow steady stream, through the opening in the blender lid, until the mayonnaise is well-emulsified and thick.

The intensity of flavors may come as a shock to some palates unused to Mediterranean cooking. Do remember, though, the idea is not to saturate the dish, whether it be soup or cooked potatoes, with oil, as we do so often with regular, bland mayonnaise. Just a little aïoli packs a lot of flavor.

If you haven't the time to make the aïoli from scratch, blend five crushed garlic cloves and a tablespoon of fresh lemon juice with about a cup of commercial mayonnaise. Whichever version of aïoli you make, it will improve if allowed to stand overnight. Keep refrigerated.

AVOCADOS: Under-ripe avocados taste bitter and astringent; when ripe, the skin is dark green and yields slightly to soft finger pressure. Avocados ripen quickly at room temperature, so if you are shopping a day or two ahead, buy them slightly on the firm side.

BASMATI RICE: A delicately perfumed rice that goes well with fish and poultry, as well as with curried and spicy dishes. It has a reputation for being sticky, but this is due to incorrect cooking. The rice must be rinsed several times in cold water to remove the surface starch. Alternatively, simmer the unwashed rice ten to fifteen minutes in any amount of water; drain and rinse well with cold water, then steam until the rice is tender.

The partially cooked rice can be prepared well ahead and frozen, cutting down on last-minute preparation time.

BUTTER: Always use unsalted butter; it has a fresher taste than the salted variety and is a healthier choice, as it allows you to control the amount of salt in your cooking. Unsalted butter should be stored covered in the fridge, so that it retains that fresh, sweet taste. It can be softened quickly with a few seconds in the microwave, in a patch of sunlight on the countertop, or in a warm oven (watch it carefully).

If you must use margarine, make sure it is unsalted.

CHICKEN BREASTS: Placing very cold meat or poultry straight on the heat causes the fibres to contract, squeezing out the juices and leaving the meat tough and dry. Any meat or poultry that is to be cooked quickly on the stovetop or grill should, if at all possible, be allowed to sit (covered) at room temperature for twenty to thirty minutes before cooking.

CHICKEN BROTH: Canned, condensed chicken broth (preferably low-salt) is quite acceptable, although not nearly as good as homemade. Making your own stock is not a difficult or time-consuming task. I make it whenever I have bones from chicken wings or a roast. Place the bones, along with the giblets and any meat you won't otherwise use, in a heavy sauce pan with a couple of carrots, celery stalks and onions, perhaps a bay leaf, and some whole peppercorns. Cover with cold water and bring to a slow simmer. Start the stock while you are clearing up the dinner dishes and turn it off at bedtime. In the morning, strain the stock and refrigerate, or freeze. Leave the fat on until you use the stock, as this helps to preserve it.

CRÈME FRAÎCHE: Cream with a slightly tart, acidic flavor. It is especially good in soups and sauces and with sweet fruit dishes. Mix equal amounts of 35% cream and sour cream (regular, not light) in a clean preserving jar. Allow it to sit uncovered (or with a piece of cheesecloth over the jar) at room temperature for twenty-four hours, or until it is thick. Cover and refrigerate; it will keep two to three weeks. To speed up the process, first heat the mixture gently for a few minutes, then allow it to stand at room temperature. It should thicken in six to eight hours.

CRÈME GERVAISE: A quick, thick cream for desserts, which can be used in place of crème fraîche. Mash one small package of cream cheese (about three ounces) until soft. Blend in half a cup of thick sour cream (regular, not light) and a tablespoon of brandy. This cream is excellent served with any spiced fruit, especially peaches or apples, as a dessert, or as a garnish for simply cooked pork or veal.

CRÊPES: In a blender, swirl 3 large eggs, 1 cup milk, and 3/4 cup flour until smooth. Allow to stand for a minute or two. In a medium or large non-stick skillet, over medium-high heat, melt a teaspoon of butter. Pour in about a quarter cup of batter and tilt the skillet quickly to spread it. Flip the crêpe when the top is just dry. When finished it should be a light golden brown on both sides. Transfer to a plate and repeat with the remaining batter. This recipe makes about ten medium crêpes. When they are cool, place a sheet of plastic wrap between each one, wrap well, and freeze.

DANISH CREAM: A can of thick Danish cream is great to have in the cupboard for an emergency. Use it in place of fresh cream in soups and sauces.

DRY WHITE VERMOUTH: Any dry white wine will do, but vermouth is useful to have around for cooking, so that you don't have to open a bottle of wine when you only need a small amount.

FINES HERBES: A commercially available blend of tarragon, chervil, chives and parsley, extremely useful as a garnish or for an extra dash of flavor, especially on soups, salads, fish, chicken, and eggs.

FRESH HERBS: Nothing matches the flavor of fresh herbs, or the look for that matter, in the presentation of your meals. Even the smallest kitchen should have room for a pot of parsley, rosemary, basil and thyme; however, many grocery stores now carry cuttings of fresh herbs, most of which will last for weeks in the fridge with a little care. Rinse them well and store them, stems down, in a tiny amount of water in a mason jar. Change the water whenever you use a sprig, and remove blemished leaves promptly. Basil will not keep; its pungent freshness is best preserved as pesto.

GARLIC: There is only one way to use garlic, and that is from fresh cloves. Garlic powder is a bitter, odious substitute not to be tolerated by any self-respecting cook. Preserved crushed garlic is little better and an expensive nuisance to store. Fresh cloves keep for months in an aerated container; buy one to suit your kitchen or galley decor and leave it handy on a counter or open shelf.

To peel a whole garlic clove, hit it lightly with the flat edge of a broad knife; the skin will fall off. Whole cloves are easily crushed or grated with a garlic press (see "Gadgets" under "The Essential Galley").

To remove the smell of garlic (or onions) from your hands, rub your fingers with a little pure vanilla extract (even vanilla ice cream, if it's the real thing, will work) or, if you're not squeamish, with used coffee grounds. Alternatively, run your fingers along the flat of a high carbon steel knife blade (such as a carving knife) under cold running water (not recommended for on-board ship).

You can get rid of the lingering taste of garlic by chewing on a coffee bean or by actually drinking a cup of the brew.

GINGER: Fresh ginger has a nose-tickling pungency combined with an unexpectedly sweet fragrance, both characteristics far removed from the dry dusty taste and smell of the powdered variety. If you can't find fresh ginger, leave it out altogether.

Ginger root should never be refrigerated or kept in plastic, as it will go moldy. Store it at room temperature in an aerated pot or an open basket. The outside will shrivel a bit, but the inside will stay fresh for weeks. Cut off as much as you need and peel it with a sharp knife before slicing or grating.

HERBED FLOUR: A useful item to have in the cupboard. Make it by shaking together the following ingredients in a small jar: 1/2 cup all-purpose flour, 1 tablespoon each of dried basil, thyme and tarragon (or oregano), and 1 teaspoon paprika.

LEMONS AND LIMES: Nothing can match the flavor of freshly squeezed juice, so keep a supply of both fruits on hand; besides, they are a joy to see in a bowl on the kitchen counter.

MIXED PEPPERCORNS: A commercially available blend of black, white, green, and pink peppercorns. I make my own, as the pre-mixed jars contain too high a proportion of black peppercorns.

To crush the peppercorns coarsely, use a mortar and pestle, or place the peppercorns in a plastic sandwich bag and crush them with a rolling pin or hammer. Another excellent way, if you have the storage space, is to use an electric coffee grinder (kept exclusively for grinding spices).

MUSHROOMS: Store in paper bags, not in plastic. Wash all mushrooms quickly under cold running water, as soaking them causes them to absorb vast amounts of liquid and ruins them for cooking. If possible, allow them to dry well before use. Mushroom brushes are, to my mind, unsanitary gimmicks and a nuisance to have cluttering up valuable kitchen or galley drawer space.

Many wild mushrooms are now grown commercially and are available fresh at most grocery stores. Packets of dried wild mushrooms take up little space in the pantry and are handy to have in reserve.

The stems of portobello and shiitake mushrooms, while too woody to make pleasant eating, are great for flavoring soup stocks and broths. Freeze them for this purpose if you can't use them right away.

OLIVE OIL: Always use extra virgin, cold-pressed olive oil, which is fresh tasting and low in acid. There are many fine nuances of taste in virgin oils that are interesting to explore; try a few brands, and learn to trust your taste so that you know when an oil is "off" (beginning to go rancid). Store a small amount for everyday use in a dark jar, away from the stove, as light and heat will break down the structure of the oil. Store the bulk of your oil in the coolest cupboard you have.

PARMESAN CHEESE: Don't even consider using the packaged pre-grated variety, which bears no resemblance at all to the real thing. Buy it in chunks (Reggiano is the best); wrapped well, it keeps for weeks. I buy it in huge blocks at a farmers' market, where it is about half the grocery store price, and freeze it. The cheese can be grated straight from the freezer.

PEPPER: Must be freshly ground. The pre-ground variety is always stale and uninteresting, and will spoil the flavor of your food. Get a good pepper mill with Peugot or Marlux workings; it will be a joy to use and will last a lifetime.

PESTO: Usually made with basil, but good with a number of different herbs, particularly rosemary. Pesto at its most basic is no more than the fresh herb puréed with enough olive oil to make a thick paste. Add garlic and pine nuts if you like. Parmesan cheese is also good with basil pesto, but the pesto will not keep as well.

Store pesto in the fridge with a layer of olive oil on top, or freeze it for longer storage.

PINE NUTS: Yes, they really do come from pine cones (Italian pine cones, that is). They are expensive, but worth the price. Store them in a Mason jar or in a freezer bag in the freezer.

Slivered almonds make a reasonable substitute.

Toast the nuts in a heavy dry skillet. Preheat the pan, throw in the nuts, and toss every few seconds until they are golden brown, usually about a minute or two. (This also works well for toasting coconut.)

PINK PEPPERCORNS: These are actually a piquant, slightly sweet pink berry, originally from Madagascar. They add a distinctive, somewhat exotic flavor to salads and sauces, and are particularly good with veal, poultry and white fish. To crush pink peppercorns, use a mortar and pestle, or place them in a plastic sandwich bag and crush them with a rolling pin or a hammer.

PORK TENDERLOIN: Placing very cold meat or poultry straight on the heat causes the fibres to contract, squeezing out the juices and leaving the meat tough and dry. Any meat or poultry that is to be cooked quickly on the stovetop or grill should, if at all possible, be allowed to sit (covered) at room temperature for twenty to thirty minutes before cooking.

ROASTED RED BELL PEPPER: Cut the pepper in half and remove the seeds and white pith. Place, skin side up, under a broiler and leave until the skin is blistered and beginning to blacken, ten to fifteen minutes. Place the halves on a plate with an overturned bowl on top or in a paper bag, and leave to steam for another ten minutes or so (this makes it easy to remove the skin). When the halves are cool enough to handle, slip off the skin and discard it. Continue with the roasted flesh as directed in the recipe.

Roasted peppers are easy to preserve. Just cover with olive oil in a clean jar and keep refrigerated. Store-bought roasted peppers in jars are good, too, and a handy commodity to have in the cupboard. Drain well on a paper towel before using.

Rose petals: Edible flowers, often overlooked for their culinary merits, are a colorful, fragrant and delicate addition to many dishes. Most are easy to grow, even if you only have space for a couple of pots. My favorites are nasturtiums and chive flowers (for savory dishes and salads), portulaca, violets and, of course, roses (for savory or sweet dishes).

Violets and roses are also good sugared, which preserves them and makes them an exquisite garnish for desserts. Dip the petals or entire flower in lightly beaten egg white, then sprinkle with fine fruit sugar. Leave to dry on waxed paper and store in an airtight container.

Salt: Perhaps not so critical as pepper, but still important. Pure sea salt has a fine, delicate flavor, not at all like the chemical taste of iodized table salt. Health food stores and many grocery stores carry sea salt, ground or in rock form. Salt mills, which have plastic works, are a useless pain and have given sea salt a reputation for being inconvenient. What you need is a good pepper mill (see the previous note); the steel works are of a sufficiently high quality to resist corrosion. Mine is ten years old; it looks and works like new. Pre-ground sea salt is convenient for adding to cooking water, and will work in shakers without too much clumping if you mix in a few grains of rice.

Shallots: Use French shallots (the small ones). Shallots have a more delicate, slightly sweeter flavor than yellow onions. The bulbs of green onions are not a suitable substitute — if shallots are not available, use white salad onion instead.

To mince shallots, put them through a garlic press; there is no need to peel them first.

Tomatoes, slicing: According to Julia Child, the definition of a sharp knife is one that will cut through the skin of a fresh tomato cleanly and without effort. Before attempting to slice any tomatoes, but particularly for tomato flowers, be sure to sharpen your slicing knife. Otherwise, you will not be able to make clean cuts, ruining the look of the tomatoes and possibly spoiling your pleasure in preparing the meal. Dull knives are also a danger to your fingers, as they tend to slip when you are applying pressure.

Tomato paste: One can of tomato paste is often too much to use at once, and it does not keep well once it is opened. Don't be tempted to add more than is called for in order to use it up, as you will spoil your dish. Freeze any leftover paste in tablespoon-size portions in plastic wrap. These little nuggets are great to have ready to toss into a soup, stew or sauce as necessary.

Zest: Most of our fruit is waxed and should be rinsed in warm water before the skin is grated. (For information on zesters, see "Gadgets" under "The Essential Galley.")

What though youth gave love and roses,
Age still leaves us friends and wine.

— Thomas Moore

WINE WISDOM

Wine is made to go with food, so matching wines with dishes should not be a daunting task. Instead, it should be one of the most interesting and enjoyable parts of planning a meal. It is helpful to have some idea about the general characteristics of the major wine-making grape varieties. The following is a brief overview.

White Grape Varieties

Aligoté: Grown in Burgundy, this grape makes thin, tart wines best used as a base for the finest of refreshing aperitifs — the kir. Into a wineglass full of well-chilled Aligoté, pour about half an ounce (or less, to taste) of crème de cassis. This has always been our standard pre-dinner drink aboard the *King James Version*; it livens the palate, rather than dulling it, as do the usual heavily alcoholic North American cocktails. (A kir royale, even better, is made in the same way, with champagne and crème de cassis.) Aligoté is an expensive wine; the thin, rather acidic Sauvignon Blanc, made by Gallo (California), is a reasonably priced substitute.

Chardonnay: The grape of the celebrated white Burgundies, this is the greatest dry white wine grape in the world, grown in virtually every commercial wine-making area. Wines range from lush, golden, oaky wines, rich with vanillins, to thin, greenish, apple-scented wines, flinty and somewhat austere. Much depends on the skill and aims of the wine maker, as well as on the climate and the weather during a particular growing season. In general, wines from Australia and California tend to be more powerful. Australian Chardonnays especially have been over-oaked, though that is changing. Ontario now produces some excellent, moderately priced Chardonnays.

This grape is also one of the three major varieties used in making champagne.

Chenin Blanc: The famous grape of wines from Touraine and Anjou, in France, Chenin Blanc is used in the production of dry and sweet, still, and sparkling wines, which often have a distinctive floral character. Chenin Blanc is grown with great success in Australia and the southern United States. A good wine to drink on its own or with shellfish, especially scallops.

Twenty-Eight Bottles Around the Bay 67

COLOMBARD: A grape that produces thin, acidic wines used in the distillation of cognac and armagnac. In California, where the hot growing season makes the high acidity and sugar content a plus, Colombard is used to make simple, light-bodied wines that make excellent aperitifs, with enough acidity to stand up to vinaigrette-dressed salads.

GEWÜRZTRAMINER: Originally grown in Germany and Alsace (where it is most successful), this grape is now cultivated with good results in Ontario. The wines are aromatic, often described as spicy or peppery. They are usually just off dry, and make a good accompaniment to hors d'oeuvres, game fowl, mild curried dishes, pâtés, and terrines, and are excellent with avocado and appetizers dressed with vinaigrette. Gewürztraminer Auslese is a very sweet wine made from late-picked grapes. In good years, it may contain some botrytized grapes (grapes affected by *Botrytis cinerea*, or "noble rot," a fungal growth that concentrates the sugars in ripe grapes, allowing for the production of highly alcoholic, decadently sweet, rich dessert wines).

MUSCADET: Also known as Gamay Blanc, this grape is the basis of the best wines in the Sèvre-et-Maine district of France, at the western end of the Loire Valley. As the grape itself is rather neutral in flavor, the best wines are made *sur lie* — that is, the wine is left in contact with its sediment (lees) until it is bottled. This enhances the fruit and gives the wine a musky depth from the yeast, as well as a slight spritz from natural carbonic gas. Wine thus produced bears the label Muscadet de Sèvre-et-Maine sur lie. It is an excellent, classic accompaniment to oysters on the half shell, simply prepared shellfish, and white fish. It also goes well with salads, vegetable terrines and avocado dishes.

PINOT GRIS: A grape at its best in Alsace, where it is known as Tokay d'Alsace (not to be confused with Hungarian Tokay, a rich dessert wine made from the Furmint and Hárslevelü grapes). It is also used in many Italian whites. Pinot Gris produces rich, complex wines that are a good accompaniment to flavorful white fish such as sea bass and halibut, lighter game birds, and grain-fed poultry, as well as light meat casseroles. It is exceptionally good with Gruyère and other hard, mild cheeses.

RIESLING: The most classic German grape variety, now grown extensively in Ontario. The wines, generally light-bodied and fruity, and low in acid and alcohol, are good to drink on their own or with river fish such as trout. Like Gewürztraminer, the Riesling grape is susceptible to botrytis. There are many good late-harvest Rieslings (Spätlese) on the market.

SAUVIGNON BLANC: A grape grown extensively in the Loire Valley, where it produces crisp clean wines with intense varietal character. The most well-known appellations are Sancerre, which produces bone-dry, medium to full-bodied whites with the concentrated flavor and aroma of gooseberries, and Pouilly-Fumé, famous for the smoky character of its wines. Both are ideal with shellfish, smoked fish and mackerel, especially when served with a cream or butter sauce. California produces some exceptional wines from this grape, and those from Chile are generally good, easy to drink, and reasonably priced.

SÉMILLON: The main grape grown in Sauternes and Barsac, in France; it is very susceptible to botrytis and is used in the production of the richest, most decadently unctuous dessert wines in the world. It is also grown successfully in Australia and is often blended with the Chardonnay grape in the production of dry table wines.

BLACK GRAPE VARIETIES

CABERNET SAUVIGNON: The most important, noble red wine grape in the world, vital to the classic red wines of Bordeaux, but now grown around the world, most successfully in California, Australia and Chile. The wines are long lived, dense and tannic, redolent with the flavors and aromas of raspberries, currants, cedar, leather, tobacco...the list goes on and on. Cabernet Sauvignon is the classic accompaniment for roast beef and lamb.

GAMAY: The grape of Beaujolais, that famous fruity wine of France, though Gamay is now grown in many other areas of the world. The wines are simple, light red, and bursting with ripe cherry flavors. They should be drunk young, slightly chilled, and may be served with light meat casseroles, roast pork, chicken and turkey, cold meats (particularly pork), cold duck, and goat cheese. Even die-hard white-wine-only drinkers usually find these wines potable.

GRENACHE: The main grape in Châteauneuf-du-Pape, from the south of France, and in the Spanish Rioja, Grenache produces rich, dense, highly alcoholic wines. It is always blended with other grape varieties.

MERLOT: A luscious grape that produces soft, velvety wines capable of great richness. The most well known are from the Bordeaux regions of Pomerol and St.-Emilion. Merlot is also used to soften many Cabernet Sauvignon wines, especially in Bordeaux. Bulgarian Merlots — soft, rich, and versatile — are one of the great wine bargains and pair well with virtually any beef dish or dark meat casserole.

NEBBIOLO: The principal grape used in the production of Barolo, the great wine of Italy; it is often combined with Merlot or a similar grape, which softens the wine.

PINOT NOIR: The grape of the great red Burgundies, producing, in good years, the most velvety, rich red wines in the world. Always a perfect accompaniment to lamb,

TWENTY-EIGHT BOTTLES AROUND THE BAY

duck, game birds, and, of course, beef braised in red wine, commonly known as boeuf bourguignon.

Pinot Noir is also used in the production of champagne.

SANGIOVESE: The main grape in Chianti. It is usually blended with other grape varieties to give it the plummy fruit flavors it lacks on its own.

SYRAH: Also called Shiraz, this grape is best known for the massive, rich, tannic but fruity red wines it produces in Hermitage, in the northern Rhône. It is also successful in Australia, where the wines tend to be lower in tannins and therefore easier to drink when young. A good wine with game and a nice quaffing wine on its own.

ZINFANDEL: A grape most successful in California, where it produces some huge, tannic red wines, as well as the more familiar light, slightly sweet whites and rosés.

On Serving Wine with Food

Most of us have heard the old maxims that have to do with serving wine: white with fish, red with meat, young wines before old, dry before sweet. These may be reasonable as general guidelines, but should never be taken as hard-and-fast rules. The most important consideration should always be that you like both the food and the wine.

When choosing wines to go with your meals, ask yourself "What is the predominant flavor and texture of the dish?"

All foods change the way a wine tastes. For instance, highly acidic foods, such as fresh fruit, tomatoes, and the lemon juice or vinegar found in most salad dressings, make many wines taste metallic; however, a white wine that is too acidic on its own will seem fuller and softer when drunk with acidic foods. A young, moderately priced wine made with the Sauvignon Blanc grape would, for example, go well with the tomato flowers in Menu Four, or with the zucchini in olive oil and lemon juice in Menu Eight.

Complex dishes that are grilled or have a variety of seasonings are best served with simple wines. For instance, you would not serve a mature red Bordeaux with the braised beef in Menu Nine, as the intensity of flavors from the combined vegetables and garlic and the carbonised beef would overwhelm the subtleties of the wine. Better to serve a simple young Pinot Noir, Merlot, or Syrah.

On the other hand, the oven-roasted rack of lamb in Menu Five will show up every nuance of aroma and flavor in the wine. It should be served with a fine Cabernet Sauvignon from Bordeaux, Australia or California, a good Châteauneuf-du-Pape, or a red Burgundy.

When a dish is served with a sauce, that is often the most important factor to consider. If the sauce is wine-based, then the choice may be easy — use the same wine or one made from the same grape. The champagne chicken in Menu Seven, for instance, goes beautifully with a champagne-style wine or with a

Chardonnay, as long as it is not overly oaked (something French or Canadian, rather than Australian or Californian). Creamy and buttery sauces, such as the mushroom and shallot sauce with the veal in Menu Four, go well with lustier, richer, well-oaked Californian or Australian Chardonnays, or aged white Burgundies.

Peppery sauces or seasonings, like the crushed pepper coating for the beef tenderloin in Menu Eight, sensitize the palate, ruining the nuances of a fine old wine, but they go extremely well with young, intense, tannic reds, such as those from the Rhône (especially Gigondas), or Chianti, making the wine seem stronger, fuller, and more complex.

It is important to match the texture of a food to the wine. Heavily textured foods require full-bodied wines (this is why meats generally go best with red wines). Fats, oils, and salt, commonly associated with heavily textured meats, neutralize harsh tannins in wine, making young reds taste smoother and fuller bodied. There are also some types of fish and seafood, especially salmon and lobster, that have a heavy, fatty texture. The high salt content, however, can make highly alcoholic, tannic wines taste bitter, so it is better to stick to a lighter, chillable wine such as a Beaujolais, any wine from the Gamay grape, or a full-bodied Chardonnay.

Lighter textured foods, such as most shellfish, and delicately flavored fish, such as sole and trout, should be accompanied by a less intense wine — a Riesling, almost any Italian white, a Chilean Chardonnay, or French Mâconnais.

Spicy foods, and those heavily flavored with garlic, demand a chillable, fruity, slightly sweet wine, such as a Chenin Blanc or rosé, which neutralizes the garlic and refreshes the palate.

When it comes to cheese, the creamy sweetness of a Sauternes or Hungarian Tokay marries beautifully with Stilton, Roquefort and other salty blue-veined cheeses. Beaujolais or a light Pinot Noir will go well with most soft mild cheeses. Champagne or a fragrant dry white is best with young Brie and Camembert. Strong-flavored hard cheeses such as aged Cheddar need a good Cabernet Sauvignon or Châteauneuf-du-Pape. Sauvignon Blanc with chèvre is a classic.

Sweet foods emphasize acidity in wine, making all dry wines taste dreadful. The wine must be sweeter than the dish. Try, for example, a Riesling Auslese or Asti Spumante with the peach chiffon in Menu Eight. Rich, slightly spicy desserts, especially those with fruit, such as the brandied fruit with croustades in Menu Seven, require a fuller wine, such as a Sauternes or Hungarian Tokay. Chocolate is anathema to most wines, but try it with a Hungarian Tokay, a young port, or a liqueur.

TWENTY-EIGHT BOTTLES AROUND THE BAY

Breathing, Decanting, and Temperature

Aggressively tannic young reds benefit from being opened ahead of time. Decant a wine only if there is a good deal of light sediment (strain the dregs through a coffee filter).

Chilling a white wine or a lively young red improves the structure of the wine while enhancing the fruit flavors. Never store wine in the fridge, as this destroys the flavor and is death to sparkling wines. Chill wine rapidly by placing it in the freezer, or in a sink or bucket of ice water.

Personal taste is the best guide when it comes to serving red wine. Bear in mind that cooler temperatures emphasize tannins. Beaujolais, which is naturally fruity and soft, should be lightly chilled. By contrast, young, tannic reds will improve if served on the warmer side. Don't be afraid to warm a bottle in a sink of hot water. Better yet, use a microwave — pull the cork, remove any metal from around the neck of the bottle, and zap it a few seconds at a time until you are happy with the temperature.

Good to the Last Drop

The importance of a good wineglass should not be overlooked. I am not speaking of anything necessarily elaborate or expensive. I mean a glass of reasonable size, not those ugly little balloon glasses used by so many restaurants.

Our shipboard glasses, made in Chalon-sur-Saone, France, combine safety and practicality with the pleasure of crystal. Called Le Taster Impitoyable, they have a unique design — gently curved base-heavy tumblers with indentations on the side and bottom for the thumb and forefinger. They come with individual, snugly fitting canisters, which, along with their base-heavy design, makes them idea for use and storage at sea. Your glasses should feel well balanced in the hand, not top-heavy when the wine is poured, and they should not have a lip on the rim, which interferes with the sensual pleasure of sipping the wine. They should also be clear glass; blue and green may look nice on the shelf, but are an atrocity when used for serving wine, particularly red.

Beyond these things, be sure always to rinse your glasses well, and never store them upside down, as this traps stale air and moisture, which will ruin any wine.

When serving, pour the glass only a third full. This will result in the maximum aromatic sensation. Salut!

Fill ev'ry glass, for wine inspires us,
And fires us
With courage, love and joy.

— John Gay
The Beggar's Opera

SHOPPING LIST

Always keep your black pepper and salt grinders full and handy as you prepare any meal, and have a jar of dried fines herbes on hand to use as a garnish on soups, salads, sauces, and potatoes.

Tips for storing perishables in limited facilities:

1. Buy meat, poultry, fish, and seafood as fresh as possible, freeze immediately, and wrap well (this includes bacon and cooked meats). Where possible, buy seafood in cans.

2. Freeze dairy products when possible: butter, cream, and milk that will be used for cooking, and hard cheeses. Do not freeze whipping cream.

3. Freeze bread and crêpes. Even bread that is a week old will come out as almost fresh-baked if it is dunked in water and then reheated in a moderate oven.

4. Store fresh vegetables and herbs in resealable bags; rinse daily.

5. Always keep canned milk and Danish cream on hand.

Breads

3 baguettes
3 loaves crusty bread, white or favorite grain
Crêpes (8)
Pound cake or other sweet loaf
White sandwich bread

Canned and Dry Goods

Rice, basmati and brown (1 cup each)
Black olives, sliced (14-ounce can)
Chick-peas (19-ounce can)
Coconut milk (1 can, optional)
Chocolate, bittersweet or semisweet (8 squares)
Clam juice (1 bottle)
Coffee, regular or instant
Condensed beef consommé (3 10-ounce cans)
Condensed chicken broth (8 10-ounce cans)
Cornstarch
Cranberry sauce (10-ounce can)
Egg noodles (optional)
Gelatin, unflavored (1 envelope)
Herbed flour
Linguine or fettuccine
Peach halves (14-ounce can)
Pear halves (14-ounce can)
Pineapple chunks (14-ounce can)
Pine nuts, or slivered almonds (1/4 cup)
Raisins, golden (1/4 cup)
Salad shrimp (1 can)
Sugar, brown, white, and confectioners'
Walnuts, chopped (1/2 cup)

Condiments

Almond extract
Balsamic vinegar
Capers (small jar)
Chutney
Extra virgin olive oil
Marmalade (thin-cut orange)

Mayonnaise
Mustard (coarse-grained Dijon)
Red wine vinegar
Roasted red peppers (1 jar)
Tomato paste
Worcestershire sauce

Dried Herbs and Spices

Allspice
Bay leaves
Cardamom
Cayenne
Coriander seed (whole)
Cumin
Curry powder
Pink peppercorns
4-peppercorn mixture (black, green, white, and pink)

Meat, Poultry and Fish

Bacon (4 slices)
Bay scallops (1/4 pound)
Beef shank, bone in (2–3 pieces)
Beef tenderloin, preferably center cut (2 pounds)
Caviar, red or black (1 small jar)
Chicken breasts, boneless, skinless (4 halves)
Cooked chicken, lamb, pork, or veal, sliced (1 pound, about 2 cups)
Lamb, 2 French-trimmed racks
Pork tenderloin (1 pound)
Salt pork (4 ounces)
Sea scallops (1/2 pound)
Sole fillets, about 6 ounces each (4)
White veal scallopini (4 pieces)

Vegetables and Fresh Herbs

Asparagus (12 spears)
Belgian endive (2 heads)
Basil (2 bunches)
Beet (1 medium)
Bell peppers (1 red, 1 green)
Carrots (mini), ready-peeled and washed (2 pounds)
Celery (1 stalk)
Chives (1 bunch)
Dates, fresh moist (4)
Dill (2 bunches)
English cucumber (1)
Fennel or anise (1 large bulb)
Garlic (4 heads)
Ginger root
Green beans, frozen French-sliced (1 cup)
Green onions (1 large bunch)
Leeks (5 medium)
Potatoes (24 baby new, 5 medium red-skinned)
Onions (3)
Parsley, preferably Italian (2 bunches)
Radishes (1 bunch)
Rosemary (several sprigs)
Salad greens (3 meals)
Salmon steaks (4)
Smoked salmon (8 slices)
Spinach (1 package, ready-washed)
Tarragon (2 bunches)
Thyme (about 12 sprigs)
Shallots (13)
Snow peas or green beans (side dish for one meal)

Mushrooms, portobello (2–3 caps)
Mushrooms, small white (3/4 pound)
Mushrooms, mixed wild, such as crimini, shiitake, and oyster (1/4 pound, or the equivalent in dried mushrooms)
Zucchini (2 baby)

Fruits

Avocado (1)
Bananas (4)
Golden Delicious apples (4)
Granny Smith apples (3)
Grapes, seedless green, red or mixed (2 cups)
Lemons (11)
Lime (1)
Oranges, seedless (3)
Pears (2)
Raspberries, fresh or frozen, unsweetened (3 cups)
Red rose petals (from one bud)
Strawberries (1 pint)
Tomatoes (7)
A few extra apples, bananas, pears, or other favorites, to prepare the hot glazed fruit in Menu 10

Dairy Products

Agnolotti, or other fresh stuffed pasta (1 pound)
Camembert, baby round
Cream cheese (3-ounce package)
Eggs, large or extra large (8)
Goat cheese, soft mild (1/2 cup)
Gruyère or Emmenthal cheese (1-pound block)
Milk (2 cups, or 1 can evaporated)
Parmesan cheese (1-pound block)
Roquefort (4 ounces)

Sour cream or plain yogurt (1 1/2 cup)
Sour cream (1 cup)
Stilton (4 ounces)
Crème fraîche (4 cups)
18% cream (1 cup)
35% cream (2 1/2 cups)
Unsalted butter (2 pounds)

Wines and Liquors (for cooking and sipping)

Brandy
Calvados
Cointreau, or other orange liqueur
Dark rum
Dry red wine
Dry sparkling white wine
Dry white vermouth
Port or Madeira wine
Gewürztraminer Auslese, Riesling Spätlese, or sweet sparkling wine

RECIPE INDEX

Some of these dishes can, with a little extra preparation, can take on an entirely different character, such as a salad that can be easily transformed into a main course. These additional dishes are listed at the end of this index. This symbol ⌘ indicates an appetizer that will also make a good dessert, or a dessert that can be served as a starter.

APPETIZERS

Asparagus Spears with Egg Mousse and Caviar, 19
Broiled Roquefort ⌘, 43
Chêvre-Stuffed Pears with Cumin Sauce ⌘, 39
Seafood Coquilles, 23
Smoked Salmon with Black Pepper Crème Fraîche, 34

SOUPS

Cardamom-Scented Apple, 18
Chick-Pea with Aïoli, 57
Chilled Avocado, 24
Chilled Herb and Parsley, 44
Clear Leek, 33
Garlic, 38
Sea Scallop, 48
Spring Green, 28
Wild Mushroom, 13

SALADS

Crudités with Herbed Dijon Vinaigrette, 53
Endive and Radish Salad with Rose Petals and Dill Cream, 14
Fennel and Orange Salad, 58
Tomato Flowers with Stilton, 29
Zucchini in Olive Oil with Toasted Pine Nuts and Golden Raisins, 49

MAIN COURSES

Agnolotti in Roasted Red Pepper Sauce, 59
Braised Beef in Red Wine, 54
Champagne Chicken, 45
Fillet of Sole with Pink Peppercorn and Tarragon Butter, 15
Grilled Salmon with Fresh Herb Salsa, 20
Medallions of Pork Tenderloin with Calvados, 25
Pepper-Crusted Beef Tenderloin in Black Olive Butter, 50
Rack of Lamb with Mustard and Rosemary Pesto, 35
Savory Crêpes with Herb-Seasoned Filling, 40
Veal in Mushroom and Shallot Cream, 30

DESSERTS

Grapes Gervaise ⌘, 26
Hot Glazed Fruit, 60
Peach Chiffon, 51
Peppered Strawberries and Crème Fraîche ⌘, 16
Pots-de-Crème with Cointreau, 31
Pound Cake Croustades with Brandied Fruit, 46
Raspberry Fool, 41
Roasted Camembert with Raspberry Coulis and Walnuts ⌘, 55
Spiced Banana and Rum Crêpes, 21
Syllabub, 36

ADDITIONAL RECIPE IDEAS

Chilled Fruit Soup (see Peach Chiffon), 51
Crudités Plate (with Potatoes in Aïoli), 53
Garlic Soup with Poached Eggs (see Garlic Soup), 38
Jellied Herb and Parsley Salad (see Chilled Herb and Parsley Soup), 44
Luncheon Salad (see Zucchini in Olive Oil), 49
Seafood Salad (see Endive and Radish Salad), 14

76 ⚓ TWENTY-EIGHT BOTTLES AROUND THE BAY

Il ne faut pas oublier que les ingrédients principaux sont l'amour et le plaisir de bien faire la cuisine.

— Jean-André Charial
Bouquet de Provence

NOTES

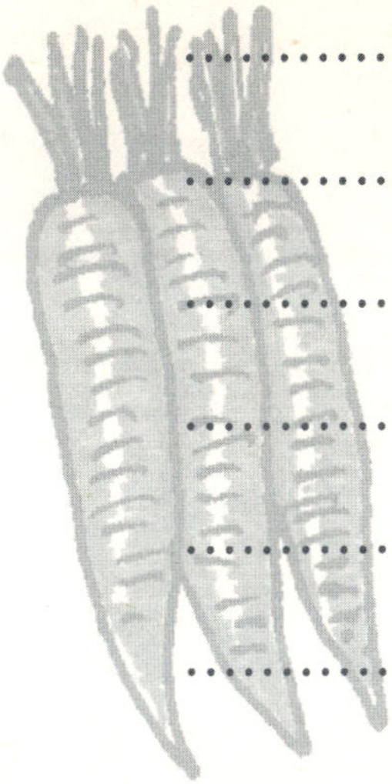

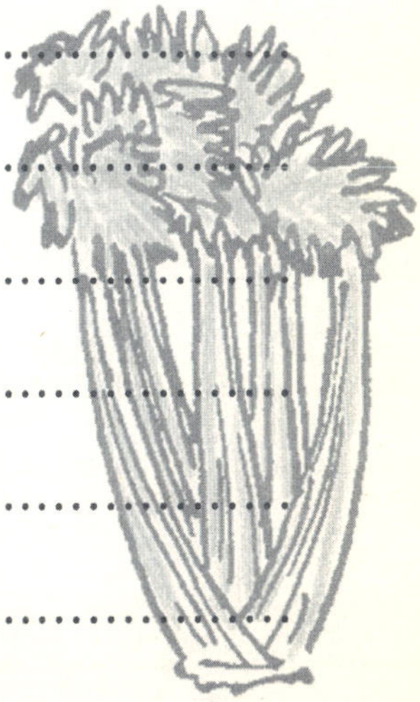

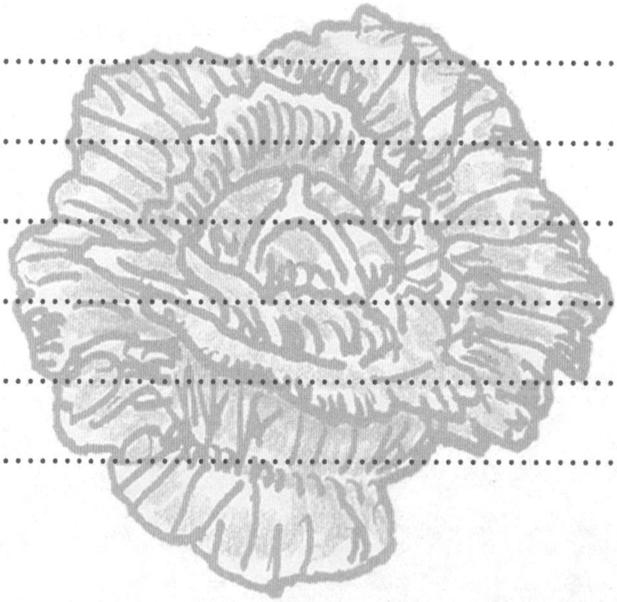